THE ELECTRIC
ROCK GARDEN

The life, the mind, and the behaviour of Indians are so strange for the people of the West that if they are described in ordinary English the books would be unintelligible to English-speaking readers.

NIRAD CHAUDHURI, *Continent of Circe*

The West seeks the individual consciousness – the enriched mind, ready perceptions and memories, individual hopes, fears, loves, conquests – the self, the local self, in all its phases and forms – and sorely doubts whether such a thing as the Universal Consciousness exists. The East seeks the Universal Consciousness, and in those cases where the quest succeeds, individual self and life thin away to a mere film, and are only the shadows cast by the glory revealed beyond.

EDWARD CARPENTER, *Civilisation, Its Cause and Cure*

THE ELECTRIC ROCK GARDEN

Philip Glazebrook

MICHAEL RUSSELL

First published in Great Britain 2001
by Michael Russell (Publishing) Ltd
Wilby Hall, Wilby, Norwich NR16 2JP

Typeset in Sabon by Waveney Typesetters
Wymondham, Norfolk
Printed and bound in Great Britain
by Biddles Ltd, Guildford and King's Lynn

Map by Leslie Robinson

ISBN 0 85955 265 9

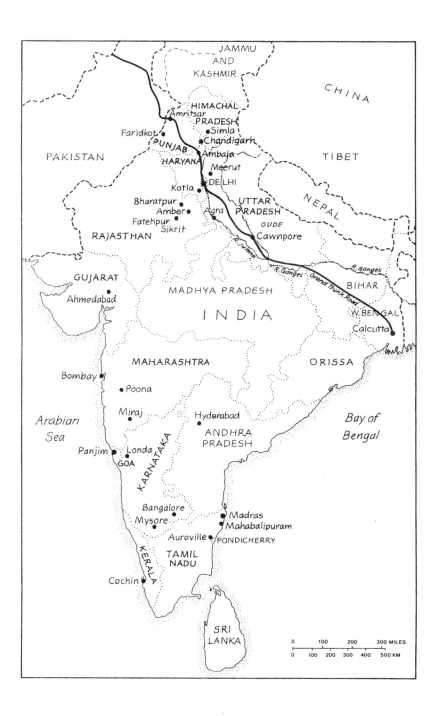

One

I first met my Sikh friend David Singh at the Pitt Club in Cambridge in the autumn of 1957. He had been brought along by his proposer as a candidate for election to that pleasant, backward-looking institution. Rather short, rather stout, rather grave, his presence faintly scented with eau de cologne, he stood his ground with an imperturbability which made him the centre of the circle, though as yet only a candidate among members. His steady damson-dark eyes rested on our faces with the stonewall glitter which concealed, in part, his disdain. Bowing a little stiffly with every introduction, watchful of hints and nuances, adding up the score as he went along – the Tikka Sahib of Faridkot was above all determined to join a club which, with all its absurdities, suited so nicely his idea of reality.

The Pitt Club even then was a survival of the pre-war world. It was an anachronism in the fifties (but, by its thriving membership, a reminder that the pre-war world did not really end until the 1960s) which had all the comfortable amenities of a Pall Mall club – smoking room, a handsome dining-room, a billiards-room, a cellar – as well as the finishing touches of such establishments: black-edged writing paper, for instance, for those in mourning who wished to correspond. It was P. G. Wodehouse's Drones Club exactly. I hope we recognised the element of pastiche as well as appreciating the comforts of the place; but it must have appealed like a glimpse of home to the taste of an Indian brought up in a stratum of Indian life which drew its inspiration from pre-war English society. To stand in that comfortably dingy smoking-room amongst sofas and writing tables, with an elderly club servant taking orders and, very probably, two or three young men sprawled in chairs in their shooting clothes with whisky-and-sodas in their hands, would have assured David that he had found the real England at last. The 'back-home' to millions of Indians who had never seen it and never would, England was a word, an idea, interpreted by each according to his notion of back-homeliness.

One of the pleasantest things about life at Cambridge was the amount of time you could devote to friendship. Indeed there were few interruptions, so that acquaintanceship could become friendship in a week of lunches and dinners and companionable outings. It was the only time in life when almost everyone you liked best lived in the same small town. In this agreeable way, after our meeting at the Pitt, David and I saw a good deal of each other. He would appear in his car at my lodgings in Malcolm Street to suggest one of the little expeditions with which he liked to vary his day: a visit to the Dorothy Café, perhaps, to watch the *thé dansant*, David apt to fidget until he had had us moved once at least to what he fancied was a better table; or a drive into the winter landscape surrounding Cambridge; or a walk through my college, Trinity, to the Backs and the Fellows' Garden. I never chose our occupation, but fell in with his suggestions. 'You drive, my dear fellow,' he would say, handing me the keys. Probably the only undergraduate who ever let another drive his car, he sat gravely beside me, his hands folded in his lap, his air that of a dignitary who chooses to sit beside his chauffeur rather than to emphasise social distinctions by sitting aloof behind. Perhaps we would drive to the Botanical Gardens, a favourite with him for little strolls, the gravelled paths suitable for the thin town shoes he wore and the neat formality of the gardens fitting in with his idea of nature's place. His conversation was at first formal, too, inquiries about my views and tastes, almost interviews into which he introduced very little information about himself. He would counter an opinion of mine by voicing the view generally held; what he thought himself about the matter, what his beliefs were, he didn't commonly – at first – divulge. Nor did he talk about his background in an expository style, preferring to let fall the occasional reverbatory remark which revealed immense things for an instant only, like a lightning flash in the midst of unmapped mountains. Sometimes such remarks sketched straightforward grandeur – 'My father maintains a couple of regiments only now' – but sometimes, and more intriguingly to my ears, he made a remark which stepped off the edge of the world. It was as we walked in the Botanical Gardens, David in one of his light grey suits, waistcoated embonpoint thrust out by his habit of clasping his hands behind his back, that he made the comment I was to remember in Delhi many years later. Turning away rather dismissively from the spring rockery he said 'My grandmother boasts an electric rock garden.'

It is a dull Englishman, especially if he has read any English history, whose imagination does not at some stage suggest a trip to India. By the time I responded to these promptings sixteen years had passed since David Singh's election to the Pitt Club. He had often invited me to visit him, but I had always put off making the journey until a grey January morning in 1973 found me waiting in the Heathrow bus which in those pioneering days ferried passengers from airport buildings to plane. It was in at least two respects the most unsuitable moment I could have chosen. In April my wife expected our first baby and, in that same month, we intended moving into a house of our own after four years of married life in rented cottages. Opposite me in the bus an elderly Sikh was busy folding up a small brown lady, perhaps his wife, perhaps his mother, gravely trussing her legs and arms in shawls until she was immobilised, when he sat her on the bench beside him like a parcel on a shelf. 'Now you stay there sometime,' the Sikh told his parcel.

Before dawn, at Delhi airport, David was waiting for me with his usual composure in the midst of chaos. 'Welcome to India, my dear fellow.' Behind him stood a hungry-looking soldier who took my passport and vanished with it into the crowd. Around us porters fought for a place, shouting aloud with eagerness to be put at work. No doubt if you arrive by sea at Bombay the uproar and chaos meeting the ship are terrific, but then you would have acclimatised to such scenes by degrees, as the ship touched at Eastern ports. Arrive by air and you compare Delhi to London. I had never before been east of Athens. Tired and disoriented, unable to see the point either of David's troop of porters or of his soldier, I kept my first views on India to myself.

My baggage appeared in the team's hands. The soldier returned with my passport and saluted. The moment we were outside in the dawn my own vitality returned, the impact of India opened sleepy eyes. There were kites wheeling above deserted avenues, dusty trees, rattletrap trucks with their cargo of robe-swathed figures travelling to work. India! I had come to see David but I was at once dazzled and intrigued by his setting.

David lived in one of the colonies, Jorbagh, and my impression when we arrived there in the first sunlight was of a plain little brick dwelling above a patch of hedged-in lawn. A servant met us and took the luggage. On the grass of the garden, as we walked up the path, two chairs had been set out under a sunshade as if in readiness for one of David's formal conversations to begin. How strange it all looked. The interior of the house was dark, the floors gleamy marble, the furniture utility and sparse. A tray was soon carried in by David's bearer, neat young Massih, a Christian from the South, staggering under tea in an inordinately large silver pot of Georgian design with sugar bowl and cream jug all flutes and scrolls to match. Almost the first thing David did was to present me with the packet of cigarettes which Massih had left on the tray. 'I advise you to smoke this brand when you have finished your Chesterfields,' he said. 'US cigarettes are only obtainable at very high cost and here you have India having a shot at making you your Chesterfields.' I took the packet of Charminar, and smoked the brand contentedly throughout the months of my stay. It was typical of David's thoughtfulness and his care, which were to protect me so effectively from harm.

A cup of tea was soon drunk, and in my eagerness to sniff the air of India I strolled out on my own into a dusty park of worn grass and trees where some boys were already practising cricket in the early sun. Part of me, my consciousness I suppose, was with me in this Indian park, but the rest of me had not yet arrived from England. Because the green parakeets and other raucous birds hide in the trees, it seemed that the trees themselves shook tin leaves and shrieked like hurdy-gurdies. 'My grandmother', David had said in the Botanical Gardens long ago, 'boasts an electric rock garden.' I'd been in India an hour and already the idea was a runner. Tiredness rubbed out my mind inch by inch. I went back to David's house and slept.

When I had repeated David's remark about his grandmother's electric rock garden to my friend Irena she had replied – irritably because everything about David irritated her – that it was typical of my attitude to David to carry away such a comment like a prize without trying to find out what it meant. Why hadn't I asked what an electric rock garden was and how it worked and why his grandmother needed one? I wasn't really interested in David, according to her – no, no, 'It's only the idea of him amuses you,' she told me, 'really you don't like him.'

Certainly David's attitude towards women did not appeal to an independently-minded and intelligent girl such as she. His courtly manner, his punctiliousness over outward forms, irritated her because she saw through them to the indifference and hauteur towards women that they veiled. He had a girl-friend, an Italian, soignée and decorative but deeply uninteresting, who appeared on his arm if an escort was needed, and quite often 'made up a foursome' with myself and Irena to dine at one of the restaurants in villages round Cambridge. David's favourite was The Bridge at Clayhithe, where he had discovered that you could buy champagne by the glass – unusual in those days – so that the panache of champagne-drinking could be enjoyed without buying the bottle. The appearance of extravagance without real recklessness was his aim, or so I thought before I had seen him outside a Cambridge context, and off to Clayhithe the four of us would set, gliding through the summer evening in David's convertible Bentley (oldish but not vintage) towards a dinner at which (or so I suspect in retrospect) he and I would talk to each other and Irena would be left to pair resentfully with Leda. No wonder she didn't like him.

But did I like him? In those first days of our friendship Irena was probably right, for I did enjoy the unintentionally comic element in David's company – the very fact of the survival of such a figure into my own era – but the more I saw of him by different lights (in London, or at my home, or abroad with him in Europe) the more sustained were to be the glimpses I had into his ancient, sophisticated and alien nature. It was not until I went to see David in India sixteen years later that I saw how aptly the Pitt Club fitted in with his ideas of reality and home. Indeed it was not until I saw him in India, and had the chance to learn a little about India from my own travels with him and without him, that I understood David's character at all. He threw a light on India for me to see it by; and India threw its light on him. What I learned about both is intended as the subject of this book.

When I woke up from a long sleep, that first morning in Delhi, I felt that I woke up entirely in India. My mind had arrived. It was a cool dark room, a shower walled off in one corner, and I could hear the television in David's room across the passage. I lay listening, taking in the astonishing fact of the broadcast being in English, and then I crossed the passage. 'Ah, welcome, let me fix you a drink.' He was drinking Scotch and took his tumbler with him 'to freshen it'. Drinks in hand, we then sat watching the dullest television I think I ever endured. Hour upon hour of it drizzled over us, Indian musical followed by quiz, then something colourful made in Hungary, next the news from a severe lady in sari and specs. So this is India, I thought as I sat there, this is what I've let myself in for, weeks of this. I knew from having English visitors to stay with me in Rome how much power the host has over his guest in a foreign land. I saw how dependent I had made myself on David. And I thought rather wryly how Irena would have laughed if she could have seen into what straits my dalliance with the idea of David had led me.

Two

'Massih! Massih!' David's sharp little distressed cry – a cry half of authority, half of dependence – began and punctuated each Delhi day. Tea at 9.15 was the first event, for which David appeared in the sitting-room wearing a camel-hair dressing gown, wild-bearded and with his hair caught up in a top-knot, somehow a rather charming undress version of the usually scented and suave personage with beard pressed into a net and midnight hair concealed in a turban of blue, emerald or rose. His beautiful turbans added to his presence as well as his stature. I don't think I had ever seen him without one until he was staying at my home one summer vacation and asked me into his room to help him stretch and wind a fresh turban before dinner. The two of us stood apart, connected by the length of stiffened muslin – was it starched, or glazed? – myself tugging first one corner and then another like an acolyte under instruction. I asked who helped him with his turbans at Cambridge. 'Oh' (impatiently), 'I have a chap upstairs I mobilise.' Friend or servant? There was always in the background of David's Cambridge life a shadowy entourage of such indefinite figures, all of them appealed to with the same mixture of authority and dependence which I heard in Jorbagh in his cry of help to Massih. I wondered if it was in David's nature, perhaps in the nature of ruling-class orientals, to make all whom he knew subservient, valuing them for their usefulness in forwarding his ends.

He sat *en déshabille*, the image of contentment, drinking his tea and talking in his low insistent musical voice which frayed very frequently into a pizzicato of giggles. Yet I was aware of an insistent dry rustle of restlessness under his talk. Even as he chatted he pushed his slippered feet incessantly back and forth on the carpet as if to clean their soles, like a man who has walked through blood. Had he always done it? I couldn't remember that hissing of shoe on rug as accompaniment to his conversation in years gone by.

For an hour we talked and made plans over our tea, or David read the paper while I wrote up my diary and asked him for the names of the people we had met the night before or the places he had taken me to. It was 10.15 before breakfast arrived, eggs and coffee and toast, and after that, repeating his cry for Massih's attendance, David disappeared into his own quarters to bathe and dress. I took a shower – the enclosure was always freshly sprinkled with insect powder scattered by the hand of a silent sweeper only ever glimpsed as he withdrew from sight like a black spider pulling his legs after him into a cranny; but however long I delayed over dressing, or writing, there was nothing to do till midday. David in these hours administered his household. 'I must quiz cook on prices,' he would say, making for the kitchen. Cook was slight and bendy and very dark-skinned, a Mug. Despite twisting himself into the humblest of attitudes when I had shaken his boneless hand, the little scrap of a man had a voice which hit a spirited note when contending with David over marketing matters. He, like Massih the bearer, had a bike, both machines maintained at David's expense, on which he toured the town's markets in search of bargains to satisfy his master. Each servant and his family had possession of a room, the bearer a back room in the house, the cook outside in the garage, where they lived cosily and I expect gratefully on the pickings to be gathered from a rich bachelor's life.

It was likely to be noon before household matters were out of the way – later if it was washday, with the additional care of dhobi's laundry list to be vetted. Work done, we would go into the garden, drinks in hand, to two chairs set up by the mali at the table under the sunshade. And there we would play chess. We had played at Cambridge. David I remembered as an unreachably secure player, Argus-eyed at foreseeing deceptions, always quickly achieving an attacking open position which commanded every key square and gave him control of the board. While the mali watered the border, or swept cigarette butts off the grass, we would talk and play good-humouredly, for David was always a pleasant person to lose a game to, and chess, which favours the player who expects every move of his opponent to conceal a perfidious intention, was a game which suited his cast of mind. If we were not going out, lunch was served at two o'clock, a walk was taken in the Lodi gardens about four and dinner, if we dined at home, was at ten. About half past midnight we would separate and go to bed, the dry pecking cough from David's room soon replaced by snores which made the doors rattle.

Such was the framework of David's day, a frame on which much social life was hung, but nonetheless a leisurely programme. A member of the Drones Club would have felt easy with our timetable. But – which never was the case with an English Drone – a considerable amount of time in the Delhi day had to be set aside for the exercise of influence, that's to say the buttering up of men of power, in order to achieve the littlest ends: a supply of Calor gas, a few bottles of Scotch, one or another of the commonplace factors in a comfortable life. To obtain such things in Delhi it was necessary to make 'friends' (in the Indian sense of friendship) of the men who controlled supplies. David's bargaining position was based on the privileges of his rank as a Ruler's eldest son – social prestige apart, the Ruler's tax-free status and residual powers, agreed at Independence, had not yet been abolished by Mrs Gandhi – privileges of which he was both proud and jealous. Although I had lived in Rome, and seen the use of influence under an Italian sky, I was ignorant enough of India rather to mock Indian influence and Indian privilege, for they seemed only to provide what could be obtained without them in Europe. The graded salutes and bitter jealousies of the maharajas always seemed a trifle absurd to outsiders. Once, on a summer visit to my home,

David – to our private amusement – was overheard saying to my mother as he stirred sugar into his coffee, 'When I assume ruling powers, Mrs Glazebrook, I shall do such and such.' But David had grown up with the expectation of inheriting from his father position and privilege together with the untaxed income assured to the Rulers under the Indian constitution. Later, the facts of political life made him a realist. After Mrs Gandhi's first attempt to deprive the Rulers of their constitutional rights, which the Supreme Court thwarted, David foresaw that she would have her way in the end. 'We'll have to wait and see [he wrote to me in 1970]. I was beginning to feel that I'd done more than enough time as Tikka and was all set to be Highness, but if Mrs G has her way I suppose I won't be Tikka much longer.'

In the 1950s David's position as heir to his father – Raja of Faridkot, a small but wealthy Sikh principality close to the Pakistan border – had seemed to his Cambridge friends satisfactorily dazzling without need of any close inquiry. If he had appeared amongst us as the Sultan of Rum it would have done quite as well. We didn't look him up in the gazetteer in case the glamour he shed on our provincialism should be stopped off. At Cambridge we lived in the present, looking very little beyond its limits of space and time, so that it wasn't till David and I reached Epernay together, a night or two after landing in France on our Long Vacation expedition to Greece in 1958, that his prospects, and the prospects of his peers in India, ever came up between us. Suddenly, abroad with David, I had stepped out of the parish of Cambridge, out of England, out of what was familiar, and I was made aware that it was he, not I, who was at home in the wide world. France was no more foreign to him than was England. As we sat drinking champagne in an Epernay restaurant – we had made the detour in order to visit 'bubbly HQ' – I felt that he had expanded, become a grown up, to match the pushing back of Cambridge limitations. I suppose I resented his upper hand. Anyway, fuelled by the fizz, I composed a tirade against petty rajas kept in their extravagance by oppressing the destitute, tin-pot tyrants who cared for nothing but the trappings of position, and had in general given up all dignity and authority to persuade the British not to abolish their pretence of it. The native states had been no more than play-pens in an English nursery, I told him. David was imperturbable, twisting his beard and letting his eyes glitter stonily at my bad manners as he wondered how he was to stick months of my company.

And, my word, we had some arguments on that trip. Once, I forget why, we even separated. It was in a resort beside one of the Italian lakes, where we had taken a room in a modest hotel, that some particularly sharp difference of opinion drove David out. Next morning, walking through the town, I saw his car parked beside the grandest lakeside hotel in the place, where he had taken a room, or very probably a suite, in relief at exchanging my standards of comfort for his own. Later, refreshed by luxury, he rang my hotel and we were reconciled, continuing our southward journey together. Much forbearance, much tact, was required of him if he was to fit within my financial scope. At Cambridge we had eaten in the same restaurants and lived the same life together, expenses limited by the same provincial ceiling. In London, his intimacy with the Savoy barman, whom he called 'Titch', had rather opened my eyes. On that European tour I soon became aware, despite his tact, of how extravagant a life a rich young man could lead in his idling progress towards Rome.

It was not for any cultural attractions that David had intended our tour to extend to Greece. The Cambridge Long Vacation lasted from mid-June till October, and he had not occupation or friends enough to fill up four vacation months in England. Nor had he the money to live in England all the year with the appearance of extravagance which he thought (rightly) was expected of him. I never knew the details of his English finances (I once heard that his father had bought a large holding in War Loan on the advice of the departing Resident in 1947, an investment which would have halved in value by

1957) but I believe there was enough of an English income to finance a handsome three-month holiday outside India every three years. Life at Cambridge, as well as expenses for all three vacations, must have strained his resources. A leisurely tour to Athens via Brindisi would take up two at least of the four vacation months, probably more, and would cost less than four months in England. Resources could be husbanded. So he had calculated.

But I never intended to go as far as Athens. Rome was far enough for me, and six weeks or so long enough away from England. David never remonstrated with me for deceiving him in this: he never revealed his vulnerability by showing how and where he was hurt, so that you could assure yourself that he wasn't upset in the least, wasn't hurt at all. And in fact his wariness did protect him from the effects of trust betrayed, at the cost of not allowing him to rely upon anyone's word. So, from Rome, we turned north and dawdled up the Adriatic coast to Venice. Once, a party of nuns singing their way along the shore broke off to help me push the Bentley out of a sandhill while David manned the wheel. We enjoyed ourselves wherever we went.

We had no particular aims beyond immediate enjoyment. I had been in Italy with two other friends the summer before and we had spent all day and every day buried over our heads in the pictures and buildings of European cultural history. But European cultural history didn't interest David. The European idea of 'antiquity' didn't impress him. India (according to that unhistorically-minded race) had a mighty civilisation when the ancestors of the Greeks were little hairy red men running about the Balkans in skins.

Even in his own land David was a perfunctory sightseer. Like the nineteenth-century Englishman on his travels, who treated the site of an earth-shaking battle, or a building of world renown, as an agreeable objective for a picnic, so for David the ruins of six earlier cities in the plains round Delhi made destinations for afternoon outings. Our first excursion, when I had been a few days in Delhi, took us to the Kutb Minar. As soon as we had parked his car among the ruins and gardens around the Minar's base, David acquired (as usual when he was sightseeing) an entourage: one or two fierce-looking fellows in dhotis who strode along with scowls on their faces, and a loquacious one-legged gardener swinging a crutch, his stump shod in leather, who put himself forward as our guide. Keeping a few yards behind us out of respect, he hopped along shouting out an almost entirely incoherent stream of history mingled with legend, the fabulous doings of djinns mixed up with Major Smith's repairs to the tower carried out in 1826.

We had come to see a marvel, the famous Minar, but what I remember is the rocky ridge of famished grass, the field of ruins, a road with tombs among broken land on one side and, on the other, building works which connected it to land-swallowing New Delhi. India itself – the brightly-coloured clothes of cyclists dodging Mercedes trucks, the families working together at bricklaying, the flights of parakeets – that afternoon it was India itself which began to disturb my consciousness by the strength of its being.

We moved on from the Kutb Minar to tea at the Holiday Inn. David with infinite thoughtfulness had paced my acclimatisation almost hour by hour, and at five o'clock on this third day after my arrival in India he judged me ready to eat for the first time a morsel prepared outside his kitchen. He ordered a plate of egg sandwiches and, with one foot in its small polished shoe tucked up on the other knee, watched me as I ate them. No doubt he was tired of Europeans succumbing to upset tummies the minute they arrived. Besides, he loved going out to tea. How often, from Cambridge, we had taken a little motor run to have tea in a garden, frittering time away over cress sandwiches under the apple trees. Was it the continuation in England of an Indian habit?

It was dusk when we drove back into Delhi, a winter dusk

with the air full of the sweet smoke of dung fires burning all along the wide, tree-lined avenues of this rich quarter of the spacious city, the cooking fires of the shadowy host in sari or cloak which seems to be in possession of India, and seems to be numberless. I thought I had come to India to see a friend, but I woke up to the fact that I was in the midst of the most remarkable country I had ever seen. What could I make of these feelings and this opportunity? Make them into the background of a novel? That was my plan.

Three

Put it in a novel. It seemed the way to preserve and utilise everything of interest that happened to me in those days: a means of overcoming the sense of time wasted, a means of nailing fleeting impressions to the page; a remedy against the impermanence of things by giving them permanence as background to a novel. Opening my notebook, scribbling a few impressions, was like opening a deep freeze and popping in the perishables. In there they were safe until wanted. Characters and story, the foreground, could come later; the details of Indian life were what I needed to arrest by grabbing them and writing them down.

Amongst the utility furniture in David's sitting-room in Jorbagh stood a bookcase of plywood and glass which held a few shelves of distressed paperbacks and two copies of the same hardback – *Try Pleasure*, by Philip Glazebrook, my first novel published three years earlier. In a single scene in the book, in Monte Carlo, is depicted a shadow-loving Indian, a figure of worldly temptation, a demonic trifler, who represents to the book's fugitive protagonist the uselessness of action as an attempt to dodge the forces of destiny.

'Si quelquefois [quotes the Indian], sur les marches d'un palais, vous vous réveillez, l'ivresse déjà diminuée ou disparue, demandez à l'horloge, aux étoiles, quelle heure il est, et ils vous répondent, "C'est l'heure de s'enivrer, enivrez-vous sans cesse."' This picturesque dandyist *décadence* was what my Indian advocated, and his appearance and mannerisms, in his one short scene, drew on what I remembered of David's exterior. But was the man's character copied from David's? When I wrote the book I hadn't seen him for seven years, for he passed through Rome only once whilst I was living there. The first time we met again after this interval he had a copy of *Try Pleasure* in his hand (the occasion was a ball given in his honour, and when I picked up the book myself I found that it had been borrowed from a public library by our ball-giving friend). If he objected he didn't say so. He may privately have chalked it up as further proof of a 'friend's' perfidy, but he showed, if anything, gratification. 'My dear Philip, I hope your prince is doing better at the tables in Monte than you or I did that time in Venice, remember?'

What the book had done for David was to give him an insight, as he believed, into the life I had led after Cambridge, when I had gone to live in Rome, for the book is set amongst Roman triflers. He took in only the surface of the book, not its argument, and went off with the idea that the life I described was the life I admired. He had overlooked the epigraph, from Denham:

Try Pleasure,
Which, when no other Enemy survives,
Still conquers all the Conquerors.

True, I had been ready to fritter away time in his company at Cambridge; true, my only novel pictured a feckless set; but how could I make him see, especially in the midst of this idle and sociable Delhi life which I was beginning to enjoy, that I wasn't really myself a Woosterish Drone but a novelist at work collecting material? Warnings I had had, of all-conquering Pleasure's power. I had seen a friend ten years older than myself carried out of his idyllic house to an ambulance taking him to a clinic in Cannes, who had raised himself enough from the stretcher to say to me 'When I was your age I drank what you drink now.' I could have described the elderly Roman playboy, sickly as Death in a masque, whom I saw every night in Roman night-clubs because, aged sixty, he had stayed at the party too long and now knew nowhere else to be. I might have repeated what the copy-chief of an advertising agency had said to me (Rome given up, I was looking for work in London): 'The trouble here with leading the sort of life when your day starts at midday with champagne in Jules' Bar is that in London you can only find such inferior people to share the bottle with.' Had I tried to differentiate myself as the book's author from the plight of its protagonist, David would only have scraped his shoe on the carpet and smiled into his hand.

It was immediately on leaving Cambridge that I had gone to live in Rome, thus losing sight of many of the people I had known. Occasionally, unusually, David wrote a letter. I find one (the Faridkot State coat-of-arms appears beside the Emmanuel letterhead) saying that he had decided to work for the Indian Foreign Office exam 'here rather than in London'. That was in August 1960. Next comes a letter from Faridkot itself, dated 1961, saying that he had failed the IFS exam and would probably be obliged to work for the Punjab government. Did rank and privilege, so useful in obtaining Calor gas, stand in his way with the examiners – were there so many stronger candidates that the IFS could turn down a man with David's education, and self-command, and languages, and knowledge of the world? By 1965 he wrote that he had been working for three years for the Punjab government (without a salary) and that he was 'bloody bored with it', only hanging on in hopes of being attached to one of the world agencies, FAO or UNESCO or the UN. Such a post was never offered. Soon he was writing from 211 Jorbagh, the news in a 1970 letter being that the Supreme Court had overturned Mrs Gandhi's first attempt to abolish the Princes' tax privileges and purses (which the Indian constitution had guaranteed to them) but that he expected her to succeed at last. Like the elderly playboys of Rome, he was one of a threatened species.

I think he looked fatalistically on the threat. I remember him talking about some friends he had stayed with in Hyderabad who had done nothing all day except play billiards. 'Rather a nice idea, don't you think?' 'No, David, I don't, I think it sounds the most depressing life imaginable.' 'Well, well! I remember you playing billiards perfectly happily all afternoon at the Pitt Club with a bottle of the '27 port by the table.' 'Fifteen years ago, David.' But in his eyes I couldn't distance my life from his. He had given up his unpaid post with the Punjab government just as I had given up my honorary attachéship at the Rome embassy. He did nothing. When he asked me what I did with my time nowadays, in a Somerset farmhouse whose remoteness he had experienced and shuddered over, I said I wrote. 'Ah, your writing.' Pursed lip, stony gaze. He did not need to add 'Then where, my dear fellow, are the books – except the one in my bookcase about your entirely idle and purposeless life in Rome?' It was the question his silence asked. And where indeed were the books? Shortly before leaving England I had had the typescript of a novel returned to me by my agent. Three years had gone by since *Try Pleasure* was published. Where were the books?

I was determined to have the attitude of a novelist, the watchfulness, the memory, the digestive power by which the imagination can transfigure facts and rearrange reality so that the world created between a novel's covers exhibits both meaning and truth as the author intends. This attitude – these intentions – separated me entirely, in my own opinion, from the idleness of David. I went to parties, and wrote up my diary, with an eager interest eagerly recorded, gleaning my basketfuls of Indian fragments in the belief that all was grist that came to the writer's mill.

He took me to a great many parties. There were drinks before lunch in well-combed gardens, there was lunch itself, more drinks in the evening, a buffet supper or a 'sit-down' after that. Socialising was continuous. Clubs, apartments, houses, embassies: we were in and out of dozens, and in each David introduced me tirelessly, watched over me, took care that I enjoyed myself.

Silence, the silent opacity with which an Indian guards his tongue out of deference or disdain for his neighbour, was to me the most disconcerting factor in Delhi society. The first place

David took me for dinner was to a marvellous Old Delhi house
in which lived two elderly Austrians, sisters, irrepressibly gay
old things with flaxen curls. In a hallway painted Pompeian
red, Italian marble columns supported Indian brassware; then
came a large long room with Persian rugs thrown down on
flagstones, all space and splendour. The second husband of one
sister, whom she had met with her cricketing first husband in a
Swiss hotel, had made a position for himself as a fashionable
architect to the Delhi smart set (though not, I believe, qualified
by anything except charm and taste) and this house in the old
town had been designed by him to accommodate his wife's
eclectic and showy possessions. After a couple of hours drinking whisky amongst the Buhl commodes and *duchesse-brisés*,
iron gates were flung open into a dining-room. We sat in high-
backed embroidered chairs, we ate off Chinese porcelain, we
drank from Baccarat – glass, of all things, was what the sisters
had saved when fleeing Singapore before it fell to the Japanese
– and we were served the numerous courses by a regiment of
turbaned servants with the mustachios of desperados. But
along with the outward grandeur went picnic-like casualness.
Across two or three guests one of the sisters shouted to me, or
responded to other shouts from her sister at the table's further
end. Betwixt her place and mine two Indians sat quiet as mice,
unaddressed and venturing nothing. It was my first immersion
in this abyss of Indian silence, so distressing to a European
brought up to believe that conversation of some sort must be
kept on its feet with one of his neighbours, and I was discon-
certed by the way their armoury of silence sank any remark I
floated to left or right. Either they were waiting, out of deference, in case one or other of their hostesses suddenly addressed
them, or they were too contemptuous to answer. There was no
conversation; the point of the party was to occupy your place
and eat your dinner.

It occurred to me that it was because they all watched their
tongues in such talk as they had together, wary of a hundred
shibboleths and pitfalls of which I knew nothing, that David

found relief from the complexities of his own Delhi society in chatting to me – a European outside the minefield, a savage from beyond the pale – about anything that came into his head. We didn't talk about books or ideas or public events; people's behaviour was what interested David.

We discussed the behaviour of everyone we knew. We talked from morning till night, at home in the garden, on the way to parties and on the way back, in Delhi's clubs or on its race-course, in every interval of social life we looked into people's minds and put forward reasons for their actions. I loved it. David always sniffed out the difference between what people averred and what they wanted. It was vital to him to know what people wanted. He was uneasy till he did, or thought he did. Gradually, as he talked, he put me in possession of a pic-ture of his own character in the way that a portrait emerges from a jigsaw. If I had learned at Cambridge the characteristics which his own surroundings revealed in him I would not have liked him less, but I might have acted more cautiously. One evening at the Gymkhana – a club where we frequently stopped in for a drink – a man approached, a functionary at one of the international organisations in Washington now home for a few days' leave, who bought us whiskies and stayed to chat, ami-ably ignoring (if he noticed) David's anxiety to get rid of him. At length we were alone, and David was able to confide that the man's wife was his 'permanent mistress' in Delhi. 'What do you think he feels like, eh, coming up and chatting as if nothing was doing?' If he hadn't been holding a drink I think he would have been rubbing his hands with satisfaction. I replied that if the man knew and took no steps, then it must suit him in some way that his wife had a lover. No doubt he had a mistress in Washington. 'No, no!' David didn't like that idea at all; he didn't in the least want to 'suit' the banker by cuckolding him. David's idea, in the matter of adultery as in all else, was to strip the situation down to its financial and strategic bones, paring it of feeling and emotion, at which basic level he liked to be assured that he himself, where it counted, called the tune. On that foundation alone was he content to build. This coldness about his heart was nothing new; I saw with hindsight that I had been given the opportunity to learn of it at Cambridge.

I have already told that David's usual escort to Cambridge parties and dinners was a well-groomed Italian girl (and 'well-groomed' in the 1950s meant glossy and trim, a corset likely to feature as a bottom layer) whom he treated with meticulous politeness – opening doors for her, handing her into his car, holding her coat whilst she put it on – which did not by any means conceal his disdain for her sex; though 'disdain', let alone scorn or contempt, is too definite a word for the suggestion of her inferiority which David's perfect manners conveyed more sharply than any rudeness to the woman whose hand he bowed over. It was what my clever friend hated him for. I too, although I couldn't help being rather impressed by David's aloofness from the emotional entanglements the rest of us floundered through with our girl-friends, couldn't help feeling that Leda was hard done by. My sympathy, expressed rather warmly to her at some party or other where we talked intimately, perhaps danced together, aroused a warm response. Perhaps wrongly vis-à-vis David, I asked her out to dinner. She drew back, looked shocked, looked haughty. 'I will have to think,' she said, leaving her hand a moment longer in mine. A note came to my rooms in Great Court next day, naming an evening for our rendezvous, and, at the promised hour, I picked her up from her lodgings in my caddish white XK140 to drive her to Royston, which was my idea of a spot remote enough from Cambridge for a clandestine date. We dined, I returned her to her door, she asked me in 'just for a moment while I find the present I have for you'. I stepped in and followed her upstairs. The present was an Italian gramophone record, Leopardi's poetry spoken to music (we had talked about Leopardi in our *causerie intime*), and I entreated her to put it on her turntable there and then, so that we could listen to it together. She consented. Of course I made a pass at her; I had by no means the success of the swan with her namesake. Emitting the furious hiss of a tragedy queen she wrenched herself free, ripped the record off the player with a screech from the needle, stamped on it and pointed to the door. I left, taking Leopardi with me (I have the record still, scored across by the high heel of a long-dead shoe) and made aware by failure that the whole outing had been rather a mistake. Would David, when he heard, ever forgive me? Next day, from David's teasing remarks, I understood that he had not only heard every detail of my evening with Leda but that he had sanctioned it himself in the first place. When she had said 'I will have to think' she had meant 'I will ask David.' The success of his counter-plot achieved two ends: confirmation that his escort was coveted by his friends, and confirmation in a fundamental axiom, that none of these friends was to be trusted.

I don't believe that trust, in the sense that Europeans give to the word, is an essential quality for an oriental to posit in a man he calls his friend. He tries to do without it, as a person crossing a ravine-bridge will try not to use a handrail which he knows to be made of defective material. Depend only on his base qualities – self-interest, vanity, cowardice, envy, greed, lust – and your friend will not let you down. There is satisfaction, a kind of comfort, to be drawn from being proven right in a contemptuous and cynical view of human nature, rather as Satan is said to be comforted by the company of those who have fallen for his temptations, and the last King of Oude by the European riff-raff he kept at his court. David's family, after all, had been surrounded by spies and toadies at least since the emergence of Faridkot as a separate kingdom in the middle of the eighteenth century, and it was a foolish and a short-lived raja who trusted his courtiers or his relations. Even by the standards of the native states of the Punjab, an unusual number of Faridkot's rulers had died by a brother's hand. It had an unhappy history. When I told one of the Austrian sisters that I was going to Faridkot for David's father's birthday she had looked at me sharply. 'He can be cruel,' she said, 'or kind.'

The more I heard David expound his wary views – marriage,

for instance, he assumed to be all loss and bother: wouldn't allow himself to suppose that he would receive (or need) any benefit from it, expecting a wife to nibble at his money, erode his independence, rearrange his furniture and sack his servants – the more I learned, the harsher I imagined to have been the climate in which he had been brought up. His was cynicism learned at a father's knee. He spoke very little about home and family. I knew his mother and father lived separately, and I knew he had a married sister in Calcutta. He told me one afternoon in his garden, as he picked God knows what substances out of his silver *pan dan* after lunch, that a second sister had married a Faridkot policeman, whom the Raja had at once sent 'for training' to Scotland Yard so as to better his prospects. But the result did not match expectations, and the family 'did not see' this sister or her policeman any more. Another Faridkot citizen, a tailor, had also been sent by the Ruler to London, to improve or perfect his skills with shears and needle by apprenticeship to Kilgour and French. But of course, once he had sniffed the free air of Savile Row, the man had never returned to cut cloth for His Highness.

From any relationship, even with his tailor, David took the precaution of expecting the worst. One day, on our way to the Red Fort, we had crossed a bridge over the Jumna and stood looking back at the city across the broad, wind-scudded water which was patched here and there by parties of duck swimming amongst reed-beds and osiers. 'A thing I wanted to ask you,' he began, as if he had brought me to this windswept spot for no other purpose. An English lady was coming out to visit him. Should he pay her hotel bill? What did I think?

It was the first sight I had had of the sandy channels of the Jumna, a river whose current seems to be the flow of time itself, rolling out of prehistory through deserts and past the walls of ancient cities. I lifted my attention from it regretfully to consider David's question. The lady, who was due to arrive any day now for an indefinitely lengthy visit, preyed on David's tranquillity as the personification of bother, and threat to freedom, which he feared from all women save his mistress safely married to her banker. To judge from the anxious way he spoke of the impending visitor, he would have me believe she was formidable. Asia shook under her approaching footfall. My private view was that if she wanted to carve him up, she would. Hotel bills were an irrelevance. 'I think you probably should pay her hotel, yes,' I said. He considered it. 'But then she might turn round to me and say "Pay this, pay that, pay all my expenses." She might think she could get a lot of money out of me.' 'OK then, don't pay her hotel bill.' 'But if I don't she is independent of me. She might start seeing someone else.' 'Well perhaps you should discuss it with her, find out if she's short of money.' Impatient scrape of shoe in dust: 'I don't want to discuss it. If I ask if she's short of money, she could take the excuse to poke into my money matters.' 'But David, if you're thinking of marrying her she'll have to know how much money there is.' He looked at me darkly, twisting a curl of his beard. 'Really, you think so? Won't she be happy with an allowance once a month?' 'Not from the way you've described her, no. And from the sound of her career to date she might have some very good tips to offer, about money and everything else.' This was met by a stony stare. I thought of what an Indian had said about the education of women: 'Teach them to read and they will be all ifs and buts.' He opened his car door. 'If you're ready we can wander round to the Red Fort.'

Money was of immense importance to David, and he managed it well, achieving what was his aim, the apparently careless munificence of wealth, on a fairly tight budget. At Cambridge he had seemed rather showy, with his convertible Bentley rushing him to Clayhithe for champagne cocktails, but it was an attitude towards wealth, conspicuous wealth, which I understood very rapidly, after a few Delhi parties, as the attitude of India. So too was the streak of recklessness which ran through David's Indian heart and threatened his European-learnt economies. He loved gambling, revelled in the atmosphere of dissipation surrounding the roulette wheel, admired the image of himself indifferently, magnificently, watching the croupier's rake as it amassed or destroyed his fortune. I had seen him playing poker at Cambridge, but it wasn't until we reached Aix-les-Bains in our Long Vacation trip together that I saw him sniff the proximity of a casino like a warhorse among the trumpets. We had three brushes with casinos that summer, and each one was calamitous.

Aix-les-Bains we reached one warm evening and, having eaten dinner, decided that we would spend an hour or so at the casino, trying our luck before deciding whether to play late and stop the night in Aix, or give up the game and drive on to sleep at another town. First we had to change into dark suits, for David was fastidious about correct dress (as well as romantic about the chicness of casinos), and, because we had no hotel room, he persuaded the restaurateur with a few coins to give us space to change on his premises. We were allotted a corner of the dining-room, which had a picture window onto the street, and there, catching the eye of the passer-by, we opened our suitcases and changed our clothes, even stretching and winding a fresh turban for David, who revelled in the limelight. Replacing our luggage in the boot we motored to the lakeside casino (you must remember there were no legal casinos in England in 1958), where we strolled through the doors very much aware of the stir caused among the greeters by the arrival of a young Indian in hand-made clothes who had stepped out of a Bentley. Obsequious staff sidled forward, bowing over their folded hands, and apologised for the necessity of just glancing at our identity cards – 'Je regrette, messieurs, c'est la loi' – before laying themselves like doormats at our feet. We handed over our passports. Fingers were snapped, champagne brought. David enjoyed his comfortable pinnacle, sitting smoking in a large armchair. In a few moments a sorrowful dignitary in a black tie emerged from his sanctum, our passports in his hand, and said that it was with infinite regret that he must forbid entrance to the casino to whichever of us was the Tikka Sahib of Faridkot, who was not yet twenty-one, whilst welcoming Mr Philip Glazebrook, who was twenty-one and two months and might therefore play as long and as deep as he liked, if he didn't mind deserting his friend.

Why did I do it? Want of feeling? To get level, having learned from being abroad with David how much more sophisticated, how very much older in experience and outlook, he was than myself? Anyway I deserted him. Saying we would meet in an hour or so at a lakeside café we had noticed nearby, I entered the gaming-rooms alone. Of course it was no fun on my own. An hour passed more slowly for me than for David at his café table. He showed no resentment when I joined him – why should he, if he didn't trust me to behave properly in the first place? – only questioning me eagerly about my losses as we drove on towards Annecy. I did not understand then that David's mentality was the outlook of someone living in a hostile society, who dare not show the weakness of trust, which places a man in another's hands. He never acknowledged an injury. When I left him in that summer in Paris, to fend for himself for the weeks of the Long Vacation which he had believed were to be occupied by our journey together to Athens, he allowed no hurt to show. Indeed, when I at last extricated myself from romantic entanglement in Le Havre and went home, I found a letter from him, postmark Paris, which suggested that my broken promise over Greece had enabled him to take a choicer path: he was 'flying down to Monte with a Swedish thing', he wrote, in whose company 'after the second bottle of fizz I couldn't care less if the whole bally plane blows up'.

Though he liked to feel extravagant on our European tour, a bit of a rip, he was, as I've said, careful most of the time to live at my rate rather than at his own. We stayed in *pensions* or modest hotels, avoided grand restaurants, kept out of the shops he loved, the jewellers and the silversmiths. But in Delhi he was always suggesting that I should buy something or other, and it was to the street of silversmiths in Old Delhi that he led me that afternoon we had stopped beside the Jumna to discuss his friend's hotel bill. I loved this first glimpse of the streets of Old Delhi in the dusk. The detail of an oriental town filled the picture: bony old cows munching apple-peel while their calves looked one way and then another like bored children wondering what mischief to make next; lighted booths of food or jewellery with their hissing flares; the cries of the cycle-rickshaws threading through the crowd; and above all the crowd itself, the touch of that quick, fragile-boned native host brushing by with a flutter of hands whose touch was like the wings of birds. Exotic to me, this (I thought) was the background to David's life. When we had walked together along King's Parade in Cambridge, stone-cold and empty under a winter sky, this strident muddle of an Indian street had been the comparison in his head. The wonder was that we spoke the same language.

In the Dariba we ensconced ourselves in a silversmith's shop. David handled disdainfully the silverware he was shown, but pressed each item on me with a salesman's patter – 'Now, I say, just look at these beakers! Feel the weight! Solid silver one hundred per cent, not like UK sterling only ninety-eight per cent. How about a dozen of them sort of sitting about on the table at your new house?' – before handing them back to the stallkeeper with the sudden recovery of his disdain. He was salesman and customer all at once, selling me to the shop and the shop to me, which I learned to accept as a dichotomy often present in the Indian character, a love of commerce for its own sake. Coca-Cola was served to us in silver mugs at our seats in the front. There was munificence, generosity, faith, in the manners of the shopkeeper as he encouraged us to handle more and more of his stock. But trust? All the while we were there his burly assistant sat between us and the street. Perfect courtesy, and perfect distrust.

We had a purpose in filling in an hour with the silversmiths that evening, for David had suggested passing time in Old

Delhi before the *son et lumière* show at the Red Fort, which he was anxious that I should see. 'You will hear some history you didn't learn at Cambridge.' We took our seats under the stars. The show began.

It very soon showed me that I knew nothing at all about pre-eighteenth-century Indian history. The lights and voices spun a past backwards into the dark, a past for the fort we sat in which reached back to Babur; battles, invaders, massacres and poisonings and elephant fights – the past for David, the structure of the minds of all those people crowding the Old Delhi streets. How had David regarded the English history he had read at Cambridge? The dissolution of the monasteries? The significance of ship-money? All the stuffing of an English mind? It made me wish I had appreciated the difference between us – the width of the gulf – rather than accepting the superficial likeness which we shared.

Then out of the loudspeakers came the events of the nineteenth century, the marching feet of the British. I sat up straight. This I knew all about. I waited to hear again how the murderous sepoys from Meerut rode into Delhi in May 1857, how the treacherous senile emperor gave asylum to every traitor, how the mob murdered English men and women in the city, how the siege from the Ridge ended with the triumphant storm and recapture of the fort, with the death of John Nicolson like a saint's martyrdom sanctifying the bloody event. This was the Indian history I had learned, an adjunct to the history of Britain. But what was this tale I heard from loudspeakers crackling like gunshots? First War of Independence? Rally of Meerut sepoys loyal to their emperor? Gallant and well-planned attempt to drive out invaders by Indian Nationalism united under the flag of Liberty? Fall of Delhi to brutal army of occupation despite heroism of Freedom Fighters? Savagery of British, hundreds of innocents blown from guns, thousands forced with whips to lick up the blood of cattle from the floors of abattoirs? I was shocked. I was furious. 'Remember Cawnpore!' I felt like shouting gruffly, the slogan British troops had shouted as they cut down the sepoys they thought of as rebels. David was teaching me Indian history through the loudspeakers, which now swept on to further triumphs, and to final victory over the British, an Independence not given gracefully as the crowning achievement of imperial rule but taken by force as the crowning achievement of centuries of purposeful work by Indian Nationalists. In the next chair David watched silently: I felt his complacency beside me in the darkness of India. He knew how outrageous this account of British rule sounded to the English, who had learned their history in England; to listen to it was part of my Indian education, my acclimatisation, a lesson best not administered by him but by the godlike voice speaking out of the Delhi sky. He was educating me through loudspeakers to make me grasp what he was like, what had gone into the construction of his mind.

I remember driving back to New Delhi in silence. I knew enough about historiography to know that the past can be constrained to teach almost any lesson. Ideology is a thrice-heated furnace in which 'facts' melt. Taught history myself first by an elderly governess in the 1940s, and then by schoolmasters drawn from the type and class of Englishman whose brothers and cousins administered the Empire – neither of them the sort much hampered by self-doubt – I believed as they did in the justice and integrity of British imperial rule. I assumed it. I assumed that the fruits of my education were that my knowledge was fact and my belief was the truth. The mind is reluctant to discredit what it was taught earliest by people of integrity whom it trusted; tear up those foundation-stones, and what building in your head is secure?

I wondered as we drove back to Jorbagh if India was going to put me to the trouble of thinking again. I felt confused and indignant. I didn't discuss the *son et lumière* with David. When we reached home, in the bedroom which had become so familiar in a week, I found my laundry returned washed by the dhobi. My English shirts and English linen were all impregnated with a trace of that bewitching sweet scent which I was aware of in every breath I drew, the essence of foreignness, of the Orient, of India. After dinner we played chess, and for the first time in our week of contests I beat David to his knees. But then I lost my advantage and gave away the game. Still, I was learning.

Four

When I had been in Delhi a week, we left the city by car for Agra. David drove: despite his generosity with any car he owned (or his liking for making chauffeurs of his friends) he wisely thought that a European should be acclimatised to Indian roads by a spell in the passenger seat. His car was the universal Hindustani Ambassador, a toughened-up Morris Oxford, which David explained to me (his tone apologetic in the light of the big cars owned in earlier days) as 'a handy runabout for town work'.

Cars were part of the worldly shell of a man's self-presentation to public scrutiny which concerned David, and his decision to forgo grandeur in order to drive a practical car suited to Indian conditions showed a concession to reality which was either evidence of good sense or the outcome of bitter experience. He had appeared at Cambridge at the wheel of a convertible Ford Zodiac which, despite its electrically operated soft top, soon got the thumbs down from the smart set. Then he didn't know what to buy. Jaguars were considered – he suggested to me that we run down to Guildford to 'buy a couple of Jaggies and race them back' – and rejected. He bought the elderly open Bentley which suited him exactly; suited, that is, the character for seemly but outdated grandeur which he was intent on making his friends build for him at Cambridge. This was the car we drove to Italy, and I remember my puzzlement at being made to stand in front of a wing crumpled in Italy to conceal the damage from his camera: from whom, for goodness sake, was he hiding it? Both of us knew, and I couldn't imagine anyone else being interested. In India I learned that an undented car was a matter of pride, colours won in the mêlée of Indian traffic. I was glad he drove us to Agra; though I'd borrowed his car in Delhi, I felt by no means ready to enter this clash of arms on the open road.

It was the variety of the traffic – the collision of eras – which made the Indian highway into a battlefield. Mightiest were the public carriers, trucks top-heavy with passengers which screamed down the middle of the road trumpeting their horns; but there were bicycles too, and bullock-carts carrying bricks and donkey-carts piled with cane, and camels swaying along loaded with iron rods, and road-gangs of women swinging their picks. It was a highway shared by every sort of traffic that ever used a road since the dawn of time. You had to tuck in and swing out, judging the speed of camels going one way and trucks coming another, you had to allow for the waywardness of donkeys and the machismo of humans, you had to accelerate into the twentieth century and brake for the fourteenth. You could have an accident in any century you chose. David was unruffled. He had no trouble dealing with Indian traffic. This free-for-all was what he was used to. When we passed a group clustered round a huge gravel-crusher, I said to him that the men tended the machine as if it lived and breathed, a descendant of the elephant. He refused to see what I meant, looking through his Indian eyes at his countrymen behaving normally.

To me everything was strange. I felt that intense interest which is like the twitch of a diviner's rod near an underground spring, a precious source. I looked at everything, bent on imprinting the strangeness of everything on my mind – the horizon of the plains, the road bordered with scrub, fields of corn and of sugar channelled by the swirling canals. I asked the names of things to fix the scene in my head. 'What are those trees, David?' 'We call them neem trees.' It didn't help. What's in a name? These things needed to become the background of my mind, familiarity making them almost invisible, before they could become background to a novel. I didn't know this at the time, or wouldn't learn it. I gazed intently out of the window to make certain that I remembered. Surely what was remembered was not wasted? There were avenues of laburnum along the road, and in the middle of a mud village a broad-spreading banyan enfolding huts and people in its shade. Here and there, decorating high ground commanding the road, were the crumpled outlines of forts. The highway was fringed with dead dogs and vultures shuffling round them. I recorded it all indiscriminately, promiscuously, like a tourist with a camcorder. Surely if it was recorded it was not wasted?

As we entered Agra that evening we passed near a secluded house, a glimpse of white columns and green lawns. Looking back I saw that it was a hotel, Laurie's. 'David, stop, can't we stay there? It looks perfect.' 'Beastly hole, full of mosquitoes.' 'Still...' It was gone, a glimpse of just that era of architecture and atmosphere I found most intriguing in India. The disappointment of passing it by was like nostalgia. Yet I have no family connection with India, no early memories of it, none of the private affectionate feelings which usually comprise nostalgia. Perhaps it was a kind of race-nostalgia of the British for their empire, particularly for this India, a sentiment I shared by being English, and detected in such places as that Anglo-Indian hotel. David drove instead to the Hotel Clark Shiraz, a rickety tower rising to umpteen stories above a necklace of spivs and snake-charmers.

It was the sort of hotel David liked, an 'international' hotel with an Indian motif, not an Anglo-Indian hotel such as Laurie's looked and not an Indian hotel such as we were obliged to stay in a few days later. Finding (to his annoyance) that the Rambagh Palace in Jaipur was full, David nevertheless toured the place with me to show me what I was missing in the matter of sitting-rooms glowing with chinoiserie and scarlet lacquer, and shaded terraces hung with punkahs, and arcades giving onto courts and tended lawns. Palace life. 'But if you still regret not sitting about slapping mosquitoes all night at Laurie's,' he said as we left the Rambagh, 'you'll be happier at Khetri House.'

Khetri House was a dreadful hotel. Did David not distinguish between its pothouse loucheness and Laurie's faded charm? Behind its gateway in the old town, under trees which creaked with the weight of crows, Khetri's was the dirty house built by a native merchant or nobleman round a muddy courtyard. It was large, a labyrinth of smelly passages. I followed David and the proprietor, a big sallow man in a sweater and slippers, down bare corridors and in and out of every room. 'This'll do me, David.' 'No, my dear fellow, come along.' What was he looking for? When he chose our rooms – doubles with dressing-room and bathroom attached – what had he found the others lacked?

I had often been puzzled to learn what rules governed David's taste, and there was time to consider it further next morning as, wakened by the loudspeaker music in the town at 5 am, I listened to the crows quarrelling in the courtyard trees and the dogs skirmishing with the pigs over lucky finds in the rich mud below them. Once, on one of the little motor runs David favoured as a pastime from Cambridge in warm weather —looking for a tea garden very probably – we had passed a sprawl of brick buildings under slate roofs, grim little barred windows issuing wisps of steam and tall chimneys spouting smoke. David slowed the car. 'Would make rather a nice country house, don't you think?' I looked in amazement. 'But David, it's a laundry.' He was unruffled, his opinion unaffected. A laundry would do. He drove on.

He very rarely committed himself in matters of taste. But in Agra he had made an exception, driving through the old city and across the Jumna to view a tomb, the Itmad-ud-Daula. For once no guide appeared at his elbow. 'I prefer it to anything else in Agra,' was all he said. It was like an inlaid casket on a green table. He had never before in my hearing voiced a similar commitment of his taste, not in Cambridge or Ely, not in Florence, not in all Rome. While I looked hard at his choice (just as I had looked hard at the Cambridge laundry) he was already in his ordinary mood again, joking abut the press coverage we would get in the Indian papers if the Jumna bridge, as seemed likely on crossing it, collapsed under our return journey. 'Cambridge men perish in bridge mishap,' he suggested for the *Agra Star*. And in the Delhi papers? 'Nothing. At the least two hundred deaths are needed for the Delhi papers,' he told me, his face shining with laughter. 'Now if you're ready, shall we be going back?'

The Clark Shiraz, and all Agra, was well crowded with groups who had come, as had I, to see the Taj Mahal and move on rapidly elsewhere. They brought to it, again as I did, not knowledge of what they were to see, but over-familiarity with its appearance. Each of us had seen thousands of representations of the Taj, in paint, in stone, in plastic and in various kinds of wood. Everyone knows what the Taj looks like. Now, if a work of art is to remain one of the wonders of the world, then it must survive all the debasing over-familiarity you carry to its gate and still knock your eyes out when you see it first. The Taj does that. You are filled with the contentment of watching a full moon in a cloudless sky. It is perfect. So refined is its proportion that it has the impact of something immense, so that you start back and look up in wonder, combined with the appeal of the miniature, which makes you want to lean down and peep through its lattices. David stood dutifully beside me. As usual --the exception was to be our visit to the Itmad-ud-Daula that afternoon – a guide had attached himself to him, an ex-schoolmaster with a muffler round his neck and rotten teeth. David, having toured the sights countless times with English friends, must have known their history backwards; did he like to be followed by a guide for the sense of entourage it gave him, a milord with his dragoman – this was how I had interpreted his train at the Kutb Minar – or did he want me to learn about India from the Indian point of view in a magisterial voice not his own? Hence this ragged schoolmaster at Agra, hence our guide at Amber a few days later, a needle-thin young man with pointed shoes and wire-hanger shoulders, who suggested that we should ride up to the Jaipur treasury on an elephant. David looked at me, deeply embarrassed. I saw that, having no more idea of my taste than I had of his, he had no idea if I'd choose to ride an elephant up that hill or not. It would have been inconsistent with everything in my nature to climb onto that elephant, but he clearly didn't know this. He was ready, as the dutiful host, to sacrifice even his dignity if his guest wished it.

If every day spent in India uncovered a little more of my friend's character and past, that evening in Agra was to be exceptionally revealing. We spent it at Laurie's Hotel. What David had not divulged the evening before, when we had driven past the place on our way to Agra, was that he knew the hotel and the couple who owned it very intimately. The barman, I learned, had served at the celebrations greeting David's birth. So why weren't we staying there? Mosquitoes, faulty plumbing, dilapidation? Or factors which reminded him of what he preferred to forget? The barman shook us whisky sours which we carried across the room to chairs by a grate in which cringed the same low fire as scarcely brightened the grate of the Gymkhana club in Delhi, a torch of some sort kept alight in the old shrines only with difficulty.

We were alone: indeed the whole hotel seemed to be empty of guests. Presently the proprietor came softly in, Mr Hotz, an Anglicised Swiss, a gentle, faded man with spirits as low as his fires. His heart was away in the hill-stations of north India watching birds. He talked of opening a new hotel, expressly for ornithologists, at the sanctuary at Bharatpur; that this was a pipe-dream was made clear by his wife's withering tone directed at all his doings. She, when she arrived noisily in the quiet room, soon gave the impression that, whatever it cost others, she herself would not be touched by failure. I saw the moment she strode in scolding her train of servants that the atmosphere she created round her was the chief cause of her husband's death-wish. David greeted her warily, his smooth condescension allotting her a place – a down-the-table place which, it was soon clear, she by no means accepted. Her career in India (he told me later) had begun with a governess's post in a prince's household, where she had consolidated a base from which to claim friendships and exert push. Was it possible that she had been David's governess? It would have accounted for the rather high tone which each tried to take with the other, that there was, or had once been, a relationship too complex to be reopened. Quitting governesshood she had taken on Hotz hoping for great things – he owned a hotel above Simla and I think others too – but his faintness of spirit had let her down and she despised him. Birdwatching! She had put away the rose-tinted binoculars long ago. Under her contemptuous eye he, poor man, felt nervously in his pockets and patted his lapels. His perplexity and confusion became more apparent with each whisky he drank.

There was no question of the drinks being on the house. I suppose that claiming the social high ground obliged David to act munificently; anyway, everyone drank their fill and David and I paid alternately, handing whatever he asked to the barman who, having observed the festivities at David's birth – possibly at Mr Hotz's Himalayan hotel, which was near the Faridkot summer residences – was now able to observe the baby fully grown, an over-stout and over-indulgent Tikka Sahib sinking the burra pegs at thirty-five with no State to inherit. I had no idea at that time how much David was drinking: not until he stayed with us in England that autumn did I realise how short a way a bottle of whisky went with him. Mrs Hotz insinuated that David's father was at one time a toper. The whole subject of Faridkot was evidently a prickly one for her to handle. 'So David is taking you there for the birthday is he?' (Despite a trace of Australian accent her voice was Indianised, a touch sing-song, and she pronounced many words the Indian way, 'brithday' for 'birthday'.) 'You'll learn a lot.' She looked at me assessingly, just as the Austrian lady had done in Delhi when she heard I was going to Faridkot. My interest in meeting David's father increased.

Hours passed in drinking whisky round the expiring cinders. I was aware of a sparring match going on between Mrs Hotz and David – poor Hotz, with whom I talked, was past sparring – in which ends were kept up, pretences kept afloat. The truth however was clear: the hotel was empty. This was the era, the early seventies, before relics of the past attained a new value in the tourist nostalgia boom, when hotels like Laurie's suffered eclipse by the Clark Shiraz.

An outdated world just before it goes under has a powerful dramatic appeal, its ruins caught in the last flare of the sinking sun. Laurie's dining-room, to which David and I repaired when the Hotzes withdrew —a steward led us to a table laid for two in front of another smoky little fire – had the twilight charm of a London club in low water. It was empty. It was neglected. For us alone its mechanism creaked into life. The steward attended us and three bearers were found, perhaps turned out of bed, to serve us our food. I commented on the number. David said 'Yes, three bearers – and you can bet your bottom dollar those Hotzes are sort of hopping around in the kitchen to guarantee we get good service.' I thought he misjudged their esteem for his status, but said nothing. He was anxious to distance himself from them – on account of their commercial decline? On social grounds? – whilst they assumed a family intimacy. 'Let's ask for wine,' he suggested in a whisper, 'see what they do. A bottle of wine please,' he called out into the shadows where the steward stood. The man disappeared carrying the hand-grenade David had lobbed him; there was a long pause; it seemed David had defeated his antagonist, if, as he thought, Mrs Hotz was directing operations from the kitchen. At last the far-off door creaked once more, and the elderly barman carried towards us over stretches of worn carpet a salver on which stood, in its half-casing of mouldy straw, a flask of Chianti. He somehow drew out the ancient cork, poured an inch into David's glass, stood back to attention; at a nod of David's turban he stepped forward to fill both our glasses and to set the bottle, respectfully napkin-wrapped, on our table. On both sides it was a ceremony beautifully conducted, the flag saluted and hauled down at sunset in an outpost of empire. Into the wine itself had somehow penetrated the rubbish of ages, for it tasted of nothing save dust and cobwebs, the shadow of wine; it was the idea of the thing, the idea of drinking the last bottle from the Hotz cellar, which we enjoyed as we sat talking in that place of shadows. I was immensely interested by the Hotz couple in their setting. They had dynamic possibilities, and I handled them in my mind like characters I had thought up to people India. I suggested to David that Mr Hotz, alerted to our unexpected arrival by his bar-bearer, had gone upstairs and tapped on his wife's bedroom door and called timidly through it 'David Faridkot is here, dear, do you think perhaps we should have a drink with him?' Muffled roar from wife. Though cross and tired, and hostile to everything his faint voice proposed, she had got off her bed and come down. 'Yes,' agreed David, 'she took time to put on that diamond clip, too, and her frock wasn't for everyday wandering about Agra.'

He knew the cost of everything, and the purpose behind every outlay. I was keenly interested by the Hotz couple, as I've said, but I hadn't done what David had done, which was to assess their appearance as it reflected their attitude to himself. A 21-gun salute? 19 guns? How many? It was second nature to him to ask. In England it was irritating, crass; but in India I saw the point of the cynical question: it was a scan of feeling, of deference, of loyalty – an essential test, on which many an anxious Ruler's life must have depended among sly courtiers a century ago.

In Laurie's Hotel all David's assertion of his position cost us was money. The Hotzes no doubt went upstairs to bed, when finally we left their premises, well enough pleased that *largesse oblige* had put a purse of rupees into their coffers for our bar bill and our ghostly bottle. Honours were even.

We were to have an uncomfortable look next day into an ex-Ruler's anxious mind. We had been asked to lunch, as I understood it in my straightforward English way, by an uncle of David's whose dwelling lay near to our route from Agra to Jaipur. But when the pile of sandstone rose ahead of us out of the wilderness of thorn and scrub, David turned the car onto a side track through this impromptu forest. We had been asked to lunch not at the palace but at a guest-house, Goldbagh, which reminded me of a golf club. Broken-down armchairs, sporting prints, pampas in a brass vase, a gong in the hall and gilt gasolier overhead: out of this somehow feckless indoor landscape emerged the man in charge, brother-in-law to the Maharaja, a plump figure in club tie and brogued shoes, uneasily wringing his hands. He was responsible for us. In an anxious atmosphere he was almost on tiptoe from anxiety. In these guest-houses (as I was to learn at Faridkot) visitors, Europeans especially, were put by the rulers to stay; made welcome, made comfortable, but at the same time made just a shade apprehensive (against their will) by the presence of the palace close at hand. His brother-in-law's proximity certainly dismayed our host, whose courtly polish immediately vanished under more hand-twisting, and nervous sideways glances, when David inquired after his uncle's health. 'His Highness is very...very depressed you see,' he whispered quickly. We were led to a table laid for two in a dining-room overshadowed by tall gloomy furniture and there, watched by our host whose English clothes looked so bold but whose Indian heart seemed of mouse-like timidity, we ate a repast of soup, fish and bananas. With the meal's conclusion came a stir without. Amid a gust of respectful salaaming there swept into the room the dark, wild-eyed Maharaja in a duffel coat pulled on over pyjamas. With long strides he stalked round the table, watched by all in attitudes of frozen piety, shooting out questions at his nephew: 'You've a got a flag for your motor? Fly it, man, fly the bally thing. I'll find you one in my palace. No trains going. Nothing doing. You haven't heard? Terrible things. Terrible deeds.' Here David tried to introduce me. Black pupils in very white eyes swept over my face. 'Who? How do you do. You will come and shoot. I am having a big shoot on the 18th. Yes, yes, I invite you. The Maharaja of Kashmir is coming. And Mysore I think. How long are you staying with me? I am leaving for Delhi immediately.' Out he rushed, his aides running behind, leaving the dining-room to pick up its timid life, the way grass rights itself after a trampling.

'What did your uncle mean, "terrible things",' I asked later on in the day.

David shifted his hands on the steering wheel, looked in his driving mirror. 'Partition.' He emitted the word reluctantly. At the time I thought he was reluctant to reveal that his uncle's mind was possessed by horrors twenty-six years old. In one such event his own state police had turned their swords on the column of Muslim Jats whom they had been charged with escorting into Pakistan. But David, although he had told me all sorts of scandalous stories about the poor man since we had left Bharatpur, did not then or at any time talk to me about the killings and madness which had accompanied India's liberation. No Indian did. Through the gathering dusk we drove towards Jaipur. Irrigated land had given way to desert and to low, hungry hills studded with watchtowers. Whatever dies, or even looks poorly, is pretty soon stripped and consumed in that harsh landscape: the bark and then the timber of failing trees carried off by humans with an instinct shared with termites, or with the vultures tugging at dead dogs, to make use of what is weak. Now and then rain fell. A shower emptied the landscape of people on foot, only the sedate bicyclists were left patrolling the road under black umbrellas. Dark came rapidly on, early on account of the rain, and with the darkness I too became aware of the persistent headlights following us which David had been watching in his mirror. I remembered the twisting hill road from Aix-les-Bains to Annecy, and David's alarm at following headlights which chased us through the mountains the night I had made him wait in a café whilst I gambled in the Aix casino. Used to Europe I had thought he was joking when he had suggested there were 'bandits' following us. He wasn't. These Indian roads were what he had had in his mind. Now I said, 'Dacoits, David?' I was half-ready myself to believe in highwaymen here. The idea of them fitted the landscape, gave eyes to the watchtowers.

'I hope not.'

'How would they know you were worth catching?'

'Follow us from my uncle's place.'

Rich man's nephew, kidnap, ransom. It would have made as little splash in the newspapers as the bridge at Agra collapsing under his car. 'Cambridge men drubbed by ruffians.' The pursuing headlights closed on us rapidly and David didn't try to outpace them. Beams searched our car. When they swung out to overtake he let them by and braked immediately, hard. Away rattled an Ambassador like ours in its smoke-cloud. The wolves had overtaken the sledge. David laughed, picking up speed again. 'Do you remember how the Millecentos were buzzing us all the time in Italy?'

'Yes.' Angry little Italian cars throwing down the gauntlet to David's Bentley

'And you seemed to be always at the wheel when one of these dog-fights came along,' he said, still irritated by my luck.

Our tour of the famous triangle, Delhi, Agra, Jaipur, allowed David to introduce me to the aspect of India he wished me to see. Next day, on our way from Jaipur back to Delhi, he pulled off the road to show me something further. He put the car under a tree and we walked into the middle of a well-shaded village square where wooden chairs stood round a wooden table. Against the walls of their low houses every inhabitant of the village older than fifteen seemed to be squatting in a trance of idleness. From staring into space they switched to staring at us – at David as curiously as at me. He asked for beer. A boy of about eight served us, active and neat-handed, rinsing the glasses in a bucket before filling them from the bottles, settling down afterwards to some careful penwork in the accounts book, his toes curling round his chair-leg as he mastered the sums. Little girls younger and with less responsibility than himself played with the bottle-tops; other children pumped up water from the well with creaks and splashes, to refresh the bucket; overhead, commotion in a neem tree showed where boys pulled off branches and threw them down into the mud square to be collected and carried to the village oven. Outnumbering these active children were the passive ones, the starers at life. A small crowd of them gathered (only children: the adults never took their backs from the wall they leaned against) and stared. There was neither curiosity nor speculation in their faces; standing perfectly quiet and still, they drank us in with their large eyes in the way calves gather to gaze at picnickers. Although passive and inoffensive it was disconcerting for a European – any European but an actor – to have his beer-drinking studied in this way. To David it was natural, unnoticed, but to me it was uncomfortable, a separation which isolated me. In a week or two I planned to travel to South India alone, and I wondered rather apprehensively how I should like it.

We entered Delhi that evening. A fortnight earlier I had flown in from London; the direct flight, direct comparison of the two capitals, had made Delhi seem a tatty, makeshift sort of place at the far ends of the earth. Not now: driving into the graceful city from its Indian provinces made me see the spacious avenues and gardens and white-columned villas of Delhi in the context of the pig-ridden alleys round the Khetri House hotel in Jaipur. It had become a capital in my eyes. I smelt the smoke of evening fires gladly, as if returning to a familiar life.

Five

O ur first port of call, returning to the capital, was the Golf Club. From there David telephoned Jorbagh to alert his household to our arrival in town. We bought drinks, carried them to easy chairs. At a crackling fire in the bar-room were gathered young men in Fair Isle sweaters discussing their round in clipped English. 'Damn good putting, actually.' Girls came in, were greeted with kisses, collected into groups planning to dine together: round the cheerful blaze in the club hearth was a vortex which the young society of a capital forms spontaneously round the spots its presence makes fashionable. So different was this from the low fires and huddled groups in the Gymkhana; or, for that matter, in Laurie's Hotel. That was India past, the old India. David's India? In his Prince of Wales check suit he could have been a father among the youngsters here. 'Remember Rome golf club, David?' I asked him as I watched svelte girls hook their arms over the shoulders of elegant young men. 'Rome...? Ah, where you took me to lunch. Tino was there, and Piero. There was a pool, I seem to think.' Indeed there was a pool, and the company of friends in a shaded terrace restaurant looking out onto the landscape of the Campagna. For a while it was the fashion. David was gratified to find Italian friends from Cambridge there. Someone said to me, 'Where's Irena?' David's eyes lighted with sly interest, or amusement, onto me. 'So, my dear Philip, she is in Rome now, your little Irena? Well, well!' The satisfied smile of one who only needed to wait, in order to be proved right.

David had rung me early that morning from Ciampino airport (a moment before the telephone rang by my bed I had woken knowing that he would call, though I hadn't heard from him for a year or more). He was on his way to London, could spend the day in Rome before taking an evening plane. I told him to take a taxi to my apartment. In the dark a hand grabbed my wrist and a voice said, 'No! Please not here. Meet him somewhere else.' Into the telephone I said, 'Hang on, David – come to Via Veneto – tell the taxi Café de Paris – and we'll have breakfast and make a plan for the day.'

So we met, and chatted away the morning, and were lunching at 'il golf' when mention of Irena made him smile. I saw his mind slotting together reasons for her absence. It was his feline smile, the cynic satisfied, that she had refused to meet. His inclusion of her in the same category as his own women was an affront. It was not a social category – that he thought duchesses in all vital respects no different from shop-girls was further cause for feminine resentment – but a moral one: you pays your money and you takes your choice. I have noticed that men who take this line (actors often do) usually chase girls of whom it is obviously true, then argue from their own case that it is a universal truth; this was what David had always argued to me at Cambridge in the case of Irena. Like Leda she was a foreign girl at Cambridge; like Leda she therefore needed only what Leda needed to make her knuckle under. To point out the differences between Leda and Irena was as vain a task as to make his Indian eye see the difference between a country house and a laundry: 'Both are girls, *c'est tout*, my dear Philip. You waste your time with sighing and writing poetry under her window when one small jewel will open the door.' This had been his advice at Cambridge and he no doubt took Irena's presence in Rome two years later for evidence that I had at last grown up and taken it. Knowing that this was what he would conclude, of course Irena wouldn't meet him now.

You draw conclusions from what you see happening whilst you are learning how to act. David's view of women's morality, and his view of the basically commercial relation between men and women, were no doubt due to what he had observed, perhaps at his father's court, whilst his outlook was forming itself.

At Cambridge, his commercial view had passed for worldly wisdom, rather enviable among the half-fledged. With Leda on his arm he looked invulnerable – was made invulnerable by his own low expectations, which my attempt to date her endorsed. My crude blunder had given him the satisfaction of the man who realises attempts are being made to cheat him, but elects to let things stand until he can best make use of the power which the knowledge has put into his hand. Fifteen years' further experience of women seemed to have confirmed his cynicism: the trouble was, he found it difficult to apply it in the case of Diana, now due very shortly to reach Delhi. He fretted, swinging his short legs so that his shoes swished the carpet, over what price she intended to exact from him. What did she want? He brought up the subject infallibly on our constitutional walks in the Lodi gardens, or on the Ridge. What did she want from him? It was more like discussing a divorce than a betrothal. I suggested that she wanted to visit India, saw in David an excellent chance to visit an India closed to trippers, and saw also the opportunity to develop, by light of his own surroundings, an understanding of his own character more complete than was possible in England. This was just the kind of specious motivation he didn't believe in, scanned for facts, dismissed. He fell back on the 'fishing fleet' – European girls who came out to India for the cold weather season having exhausted every possibility in the London marriage market, in the hopes of picking up an unsuspecting husband. Was there something held against Diana in London? Had I heard any gossip? What did she want from him, in terms he could understand? The more she wants from you the better, I said, the stronger your hand. But he didn't like not knowing in advance what she meant to take. The trouble with suspicion, the expectation of treachery, is that it cannot be turned on and off at will.

In the Indian sky there is not the occasional large hawk sailing, as you might see a buzzard or two in an English sky, but an omnipresence of vultures and kites circling on black wings, small as dots, innumerable as the stars. The harder you look, the more you see. Like the dead dogs on the highway and the stripped trees beside it, the scavengers in the sky are a reminder of what happens when things go wrong. Under this Indian sky I saw David's distrust, a wariness which had seemed to shrivel his heart in England, as an attitude he shouldn't reform even if he could. Maybe all Indians, especially the rich, are aware of the closeness of disaster – sudden collapse, destruction of hopes, failure to survive – with a vividness which Europe has tempered. David's family was rich, but how secure? He told me that of the 276 princely families 10 or 15 were unaffected financially by the perfidious abolition of their government purses, 100 more could live on in some style off their capital, and the rest were ruined. It was only a question of time before remaining privileges and exemptions were terminated likewise. But David wasn't resentful, wasn't up in arms against a faithless government. He expected treachery.

One day a tyre went flat. Every garage was a makeshift workshop outside which was posted the word PUNCHERS. We stopped at one, we stopped at two: in each David examined their stock of inner tubes, eagerly shown, and rejected them all. 'What's wrong with that one, David?' I asked, getting bored. 'See the split? Wouldn't last five minutes.' He wasn't surprised or angry that they tried to palm off old cracked tubes as new; they weren't impatient with him for taking time to discover their fraud. It was the way business was done. It was his attitude to the English Arrival. The other fellow was always up to some piece of sharp practice behind your back if you didn't watch him like a hawk. It took ages to find a garage he trusted. I began to understand why David had looked in every bedroom in Khetri House, just in case. I began to understand why he was so hard to beat at chess.

Daily life in Delhi began to make me understand, too, how clear-sightedly the English Arrival would need to look, and how thoroughly she would need to reflect, before choosing to live in India as David's wife. We went to any number of parties that week, and I enjoyed them. I was learning the ropes – the formality, the elitism, the questions about England designed to show off the questioner's familiarity with 'UK' – but it was as an outsider, a watching stranger, that I enjoyed myself, not as someone with a place at the table which needed guarding, and fighting for, every minute of the day. Even so it was exhausting, the social life of the capital, and living in it made England seem desperately remote: more remote to me than to many of these off-key Anglophiles, who had invented amongst them an England I did not know. At a 'sit-down black tie' (less usual than a buffet) I was listening to the wife of the Turkish ambassador speak about her brother, at college in England. 'He is at Sussex,' she told me, adding doubtfully, 'is that at Birmingham?' 'Not Birmingham,' cut in her husband, a big heavy Turk watching us across the table, 'Beegwood. You know Beegwood, Mr Glazebrook?' 'I'm afraid not, Excellency.' They had spirited away my England, and substituted their own.

We often played several games of chess when we came in from these parties – as well as playing outdoors under the garden umbrella before guests arrived for drinks or lunch. My game improved, playing against him was teaching me how his mind worked, but I never expected to win. At night my head was full of trapped bishops and sacrificed pawns struggling under the net of hindrance and oppression which David cast over my men.

And then at last I did win a game, delivering the killer punch cleanly where it was needed, from the superior position I'd several times established only to throw it away. I triumphed, but cautiously – it seemed to reverse our roles for me to win at games. I remembered how very careful the courtiers of the last King of Oude had been to make sure His Highness never lost a game. I needn't have worried, David was unruffled, a merry loser. Pushing away the board with a rueful sigh he said 'Tomorrow back to King's pawn gambit for Singo.' It was what people at Cambridge had called him behind his back. 'Singo' to my ear sounded faintly derisive, but probably David (whose 'real' name was Harmohinder anyway) took any pet-name for a compliment.

The day following my historic first win at the chess board was, as it happened, Republic Day. By the time we had drunk our bed-tea, and Massih had carried in breakfast, the parade from India Gate down Rajpath to Viceregal Lodge was already under way on television. 'We should have been there, David.' He shook his head, top-knot jiggling. 'Too hot. We are going to take tea with His Excellency the President, don't forget. Keep our powder dry. The parade you look at better on TV. Watch.' He left me to take his bath.

He left me to watch his country banging its chest. Down a triumphal way built by India's ex-rulers marched infantry and cavalry, tanks and elephants, with all the thump and glitter of military might. Under a hot sky, powdered by the dust of marching boots, the poor of Delhi watched their present rulers pass in glory. Twenty-five per cent of the national budget was spent at that time on arms. The generals were frightened of China, belligerent towards Pakistan, nervous of the numbers in an Indian mob – of the potential mob-horrors contained in a multitude like this one gathered to watch their masters rattle the sabre. Down the old imperial way marched a nation twenty-six years old and armed to the teeth.

Behind the military followed a train of floats. Because the commentary was in English I had no difficulty understanding how anti-British was the intention of the passing tableaux. In the back of the leading lorry the Mutiny was represented by a single scene, a nearly naked Indian tied to the muzzle of a cannon, round him a ring of Europeans in pith helmets and tight tunics with whips or guns in their hands. There followed behind this lorry others displaying similar scenes – the Amritsar massacre of course, Cowan's murder of his prisoners at Kotla in 1872, and a number of incidents I didn't recognise in which music-hall Britishers in topis and baggy shorts set about the natives with stick and pistol. The crawling snake of lorries was a pageant designed to establish the plausibility of India's history as a continuous Freedom Fight from 1857 to 1947. Each tableau was a vertebra in the reptile's backbone. Because of the visual linkage of lorry succeeding lorry, the watcher assumed a causal linkage between one incident, one tableau, and the next; a plan, an objective, a crusade. After ninety years of determined and coherent campaigning the heroes and martyrs of India had won for their mother country Freedom and Nationhood – and this thumping great army of its own was marching past to tell India to believe it.

It was propaganda from experts. No martial music accompanied the procession of British crimes, only the tramp of the oppressor's boots and the crash of a firing-squad's rifles issuing from loudspeakers. It was propaganda, but India had taken herself in, so that the show was convincingly sincere. It was like watching the Christmas Story staged by monks.

I had learned a little bit more about India, from David's company as much as from my own observation, and I was less affronted by this Indian version of history than I had been by the Red Fort's rendition of it a couple of weeks earlier. I was interested by the sincerity of the propagandists. (I hadn't then heard my own children tell an incident from their childhood in a contrary sense to my own memory of it; usually in order to show up as an injustice some action of mine which I remember as scrupulously fair.) People have the right to make up a past they can live with. Nations in the same way construct as best they can, from the material available, a version of the past which leaves them their self-esteem. By the time I watched the procession of anti-British floats crawl down the Rajpath I was ready to concede India's right to make up her own history, recapturing from the British the past as well as the present, even reconquering her cities by renaming them with native names no one could remember to use.

Anyway, whatever your intention, you can't fit the whole truth on a float, not on a hundred floats. Each tableau may be accurate in itself yet so limited that it is misleading. Take

Amritsar: in that north Indian city, in April 1919, five English-men had been murdered and a missionary, an Englishwoman, dragged off her bike and pulled half to pieces. A mob armed with lathis, the dread Indian mob, had gathered in the Jallian-walla gardens to cheer seditious demagogues. Fear of a sudden uprising followed by massacre was (wrote Nirad Chaudhuri in *Continent of Circe*) 'the product of the Mutiny which left an acute anxiety-neurosis as a permanent legacy to the British in India'. General Dyer, in charge of this terrifying situation, believed he had the first incident of another Mutiny on his hands. Remembering how the dotard Hewitt had been casti-gated for his failure to catch and crush the Meerut mutineers in May 1857 – 'old booby could have stopped the whole shoot-ing-match before it started if he'd only kept his sepoys from getting to Delhi' – Dyer acted decisively. He fired on the crowd. The Jallianwalla massacre happened. As depicted on the float, the awful event took place. It is not the whole truth, because it depicts the fact without its circumstances, but a half-truth is all there's room for on the back of a lorry – and all there is need for in a patriot's mind.

My inclination is to think well, not of Dyer's action, but of his motive. I understand why he believed an immediate armed response to the mob and its murders was essential, and why he marched armed men into the square, even why he ordered them to level their rifles against the crowd. I can understand every-thing about the incident that was not on the float. But to give the command 'Fire!' – to give Gurkhas and Baluchis the chance to fire at an Indian crowd! No, in order to pretend to under-stand that you have to fall back on bluster – 'India a powder keg, Dyer a hero to anyone who knew what they were talking about' – and still you can't forgive him. The bit on the float is the unforgivable bit.

And why should Indians think well of English motives, when they think so ill of each other's? The method by which the British assembled an Indian empire – making district after district safe for revenue-collecting and for trade – was so effective that only the British can believe it all happened more or less by accident, conquest of the entire subcontinent turning out to be the only means of securing the Company's commercial activities. Indians look into British heads and find their own devious motives there. The geographical or scientific curiosity of English travellers in India always made the native chieftains along their line of march feel uncomfortable; it was not a motive for leaving home that they could understand, or feel in their own breasts, and so they would not believe it of other men. Compass, sextant, much asking of questions and making of maps and sketching and writing down – what was this? Abstract knowledge? No. The *feringhee* came (they concluded) in order to spy out the land in search of what the native chief himself most desired to find: gold. To increase personal wealth by the discovery of gold was the only motive he could believe in (apart from pilgrimage) for making a journey. And it can't be denied that commercial interests, more complex than gold-digging but with the same intent, were always an element in the multifarious penetration of every corner of India by the wonderful curiosity and enterprise of the Eastern travellers of the nineteenth century: the native chieftain could point to the results of these 'scientific expeditions' to justify his initial cynicism when Bokhara Burnes or Moorcroft or one of the Frasers had first wandered into his territory claiming that he desired only to be allowed to measure the breadth of the river and he would go away content. If the *feringhee* swore that he did not seek 'treasure' then the raja had his own means of contradicting him. Gold, or perhaps a little emerald, would be concealed in a loaf, and the loaf presented to the lordly Englishman. Though he said he would accept neither presents nor bribes, he could not turn down this symbol of hospitality. Once he had touched the bread, signifying acceptance, the loaf would be hurried away whilst the raja smiled into his beard at the rightness of his own judgement and the universality of corruption. As the Englishman withdrew (possibly walking backwards in line with court etiquette) the ruler would murmur to his dewan 'He has taken our gold. He is putty in our hands.'

Mistrust of avowed motives, the expectation of deviousness, the anticipation of treachery, and, above all, the rewriting of history: these are the weapons an oriental arms himself with before treating with a neighbour; why should he lay them down when treating with an Englishman?

When I was young and a smoker I used to carry my matches in a little silver case. I lost it in the course of the European trip David and I made together in a Long Vacation, grieved its loss for a while, then forgot it. Like so many affectations, it was a nuisance, holding too few matches, the serrated striker dulled by use. About ten years later David took my little silver case out of his waistcoat pocket and showed it to me. 'You see I still have your present,' he said, adding discontentedly, 'though I don't sort of seem to use it.' I was too surprised to say at once that I had never given it to him; and once the moment had passed, my silence confirmed the silver trifle into his ownership. He had taken it, or picked it up somewhere I had dropped it, and he had kept it until the facts of its history had actually altered themselves to agree with his wishes. I am not complaining. He gave noble presents himself. Exasperated by the trench-coat I wore over my pyjamas at our leisurely breakfasts in Jorbagh, he presented me with a beautiful dressing-gown of mustard-coloured silk, light as a cobweb, which has been with me on my travels ever since. In retrospect (given a coarser, padded gown by a Soviet official in Tashkent) I have wondered if, more than a straightforward gift in the English sense, David's present was intended to convey the idea of the *khalat*, the dress of honour with which the Eastern nobleman invests his supplicant visitor. That was certainly the message which came with the Tashkent garment.

That afternoon David took me to the President's tea-party at

Rashtrapati Bhavan, Lutyens's Viceregal Lodge, 'whose proportions [the guide book rightly says] are quite unstinting'. The tea too was unstinting, tea outdoors on the grand scale, apotheosis of all the rain-threatened outdoor teas I had eaten with David among the rickety chairs of English orchards. Here was a Moghul garden sharp with the fastidious shapes of clipped trees, straight walks, stone vases, the brightly painted soldier placed on each corner making the whole scene look like a beautifully made board game which someone very grand indeed at the palace windows above us – and he alone – knew how to play. The idea of an electric rock garden came back into my mind. Here any wonder seemed possible.

There were guests in hundreds. There were glossy grand Indians progressing over lawns with their court circling them, there were foreign diplomats in groups, and minor bigwigs, and occasional ragged souls representing Democracy, and a great many more generals than you would think were needed. Through the crowd, behind a bow-wave of aides, rushed Mrs Gandhi in her usual hurry. On his crimson and gilt sofa the portly President nodded among his cushions, representative of the authority hidden in the long stone façade above him, delegate of the hidden power which understood the game. In hollow spaces in the crowd we met acquaintances, sipped tea, chatted with generals. Food was eagerly sought, the attendants' trays soon stripped, like the trees along the highways. Women crowded cakes onto their plates with quick looters' fingers, men ate voraciously, fragments of icing clinging to their moustaches. It was hot, the sun tiring. News kept reaching us by word of mouth that there was a foreign lady, another European, on my track somewhere in the garden; it rather irritated David for some reason, who complained 'It's as if they are wanting to serve this woman up hot for you, like a muffin.' When she appeared I found I knew her, or had known her, long ago in Rome. It was rather a relief to walk off into the garden together; the recognition of kinship with another European made me realise what a comfortable and restorative relationship such kinship is amongst a foreign race.

The garden is vast. We explored down jasmine alleys into sunken rose gardens, through open doors into silent walled spaces where even the noise of the crowd we had left did not penetrate. So far from the house the garden had remained English, trees and grass, a place of shadows. I had told my friend about the electric rock garden, and our expedition had been made in hopes of finding one, or its remains. Not here, we agreed under the shady trees. We listened to the distant parakeet-like shriek of the tea party, the thump and tootle of the band. Rather reluctantly we turned to face it. 'Maybe the whole thing's an electric rock garden,' she suggested, 'everything, the whole place.' I took in that possibility. 'Certainly Faridkot,' she said. 'Let me know how the "brithday party" goes.' When I had told her that David and I were leaving tomorrow for Faridkot to keep his father's birthday she had looked at me curiously, as others in Delhi had done, rather the way the inn-keeper raises his lantern to look curiously at the benighted traveller who appears out of the storm to inquire the way to Castle Dracula.

We walked back together to the gaudy Moghul terraces, and, as we parted, India closed over our heads again.

Six

We left Jorbagh about eleven o'clock (cook and bearer turned out to se us off, Massih bowing, the Mug wiping his hands on his apron, the two of them side by side on the step providing an impression of the young master setting out from a loyal home) and were soon driving into the flatlands of Haryana along a road planted with avenues of sheesham and neem. In an ocean of green wheat glinted the sinister whitish islands of ground made sterile by salination, the curse which follows upon the short-term blessing of irrigation – the same affliction which lays waste the hopeless landscape of Central Asia, where the attempt was made to extend (by means of irrigation) the oases of Bokhara and Samarkand. By Uzbeks the catastrophe was blamed on Moscow, on Soviet orders to increase the cotton production of the region at whatever cost. Here David blamed the British. But the intention behind irrigation, I argued, isn't malign, it's kindly. In Central Asia at first it pushed back the desert of Kyzil Kum, just as in North India it extended the wheat-growing lands. The motives of the irrigators were progressive. If they didn't know enough about eventual consequences, nor did anyone else. No one is to blame.

David wouldn't allow that. He stuck to his view, insisting that North India had been used by the British as a laboratory to try out boffins' experiments. Like one of the anti-British floats in yesterday's parade, he made no room for motives or circumstances, just room enough for the unhappy result.

I stopped arguing and watched the traffic. Here indeed was a parade, the moving crowd of an Indian road, a multifarious pageant illustrating India's history. Here were floats which had not been tampered with by ideologists. Bullock-carts followed camel-trains, bicycles overtook donkeys, walkers pegged along in the dust. In and out of the traffic dashed the public carriers, trucks bulging with people, their bonnets garlanded with marigolds, and down the road's centre tore the buses, deviating for no one, relying for safety on the tokens of good fortune daubed on their radiators. I saw in the chaos what I hadn't perceived in the traffic on our way to Agra, that every epoch in the history of road transport in India was represented. But – and this is the point – they were all sharing a road now, today, in the present time. Nothing had been superseded. Every epoch was hurtling down the same road together. Nothing was out of date. It all existed pell-mell today. There is no linear history in India.

Take the stonebreakers. There by the road they crouch, whole families, each one tap-tapping with a hammer at the hill of stones to break them into the sizes wanted by the road-mender. Now, there is in Birmingham City Art Gallery a nineteenth-century painting of a stonebreaker by Henry Wallis which is the image of despair: exhausted and dejected, the labourer has almost been reabsorbed into the earth and stone of his surroundings, dust crushed back into dust by the harshness of life, only his outline left to remind us of his humanity. It is a marvellous and moving picture, but it is a nineteenth-century picture, tied to its time. There are no more stonebreakers on English roads. Soul-crushing in that particular form is over. It has its place in history as it might have its float in a pageant. With the development of transport came roads, with roads came the stonebreakers, with further development the stonebreaker disappeared. He is part of linear history. So, in England, is the bullock-cart, and the gentleman's gig. They came and went, links in the causal chain brought about by development – by the idea of progress.

The Indian tradition is not for linear history, not for development, not for the supersession of past by present. By Indians the idea of progress was unthought of: the wheel turned, but never advanced. In early Indian history there are neither facts nor chronology, no Book of Kings, no Herodotus, no Livy, only legends and fables. On every page of an account of India before the eleventh century will be found sentences beginning 'Nothing definite is known' or 'We lack all records' or 'The scanty evidence suggests', for until the conquest of most of the subcontinent by the Turks in the eleventh century (a despotism which lasted until Tamerlane sacked Delhi in 1396), very little record of past or present was kept, so that any history of India is a speculative and tentative affair dealing in shadowy events impossible to date, and legends impossible to systematise into a chronology. The past was never sufficiently distinct an entity to be over. It isn't over now. You have only to experience India's roads to see the way past and present muddle along together.

This want of verifiable records, this melting together of legend and fact, this difficulty in trying to separate one epoch from another, was what seemed so unsatisfactory to the capacious and orderly mind of Macaulay when he decided on the direction to be taken by education in India. He found 'medical doctrines, which would disgrace an English farrier – astronomy, which would move laughter in girls at an English boarding school – history, abounding in kings thirty feet high, and reigns thirty thousand years long – and geography made up of seas of treacle and seas of butter': where was the use of teaching such stuff as that? Better to acquaint Indian children with history that was verifiable, which had a linear chronology, which showed by the development of one epoch out of its predecessor that there was a purpose inherent in the historical process – in short, better teach them history which enshrined (among the liberals of Macaulay's day) a thoroughly un-Indian concept, the idea of progress.

It was the conservatism of India, of poor Indians as well as their feudal masters, which shocked British liberals by rejecting their benevolent reforms. The Mutiny, some say, was a counter-revolution by the conservative *talukdars* and peasantry of North India to overturn the benefits – justice, security, fair taxation, land tenure, education, stability – bestowed on them by

English liberals, in favour of a return to the old unjust ways which had suited their fathers, especially in the kingdom of Oude. It was a protest against the benefits of English reforms.

It isn't with Macaulay's motivation that you can quarrel, if you look at his intentions fairly in the context of his Eurocentric and self-confident day. He wanted for Indian children the same blessings which he believed education secured for English children. It would create a class which could act as 'interpreters between us and the millions whom we govern; a class of persons Indian in blood and colour, but English in taste, in opinions, in morals and in intellect'. Such an interpreter, such a hybrid, existed in David driving me through Haryana towards his home. I don't know what Macaulay would have made of him. To me he was an interpreter, in the sense that by looking into him I found explanations of India and its puzzles.

David had read History at Cambridge. The Rise of the Tudors, The Glorious Revolution. Did he rate a book by R. H. Tawney a superior source of historical truth to Percy's *Reliques*, or were they all seas of butter alike? He certainly never learnt to apply to his own life the discipline of thinking historically, thinking in terms of linear development from cause to effect, thinking logically; nor did he even try to rid himself of self-deceptions. On our drive towards Faridkot we had stopped at the Wistling [*sic*] Teal for lunch, where David (as he ordered drinks and a large meal) told me complacently of his satisfactory visits to his London doctor. On his triennial trips to England he would undergo 'full health-check'. The doctor would say 'You are two stone overweight, you drink too much, you smoke too heavily, if you don't mend your ways you won't live beyond forty.' Indignantly (for this is not what a doctor in India would tell a rich raja's son), David would run off to some sycophantic friend, one of the court circle kept for such purposes, and ask 'Am I too fat? Do I drink too much? How many cigarettes do you think I smoke in the day?' Listening to the harmony of their answers he adds 'And anyway I'm only thirty-five, plenty of time till I'm forty.' There was no arguing with this point of view, though I tried to point out its flaws. I suppose that the admirable fatalism of orientals, the way a Turk of the old time would send for a carpet so that he might sit comfortably to watch his *yali* burn to the ground, is built upon a mind (and upon a political system) which does not make a connection between the dropped candle and the burning house. 'The doctor says I'm fine for five years.' 'But, David, that's not what he meant.' His eyes went stony as he switched them off. Lunch at the Wistling Teal, a government rest-house, was rather a snappish meal – not as snappish as dinner at Epernay long ago, but getting on that way.

I wonder now, looking back, if it wasn't our destination throwing its shadow upon him that overcast his mind as we drew nearer to Faridkot. The stranger has no idea what stress and strains a son undergoes approaching home: the son hardly knows himself, beyond a general unease. 'Childe Roland to the dark tower came.' I have always supposed the tower was once poor Roland's home, and was still his father's dwelling place.

Twenty miles from our destination – perhaps on what had once been the frontier of Faridkot State – David pulled into a garage and stopped the car. He sat without moving. Two or three men and a boy tumbled out of the shanty, salaamed, opened the car door and hurried him inside, running and chattering around his grave figure like worshippers hurrying an image into their temple. He was gone perhaps ten minutes. He re-emerged wearing a tweed suit amid the same bustling group. He had changed. Shooting his wrists out of his shirt-cuffs, and leaning forwards to avoid splashing his shoes, he suffered the boy to pour water over his hands from a kettle. So far as I could see, he hadn't spoken to any of them. Escorted to the car, he climbed in exuding eau de cologne from beard and clothes, popped a peppermint in his mouth and drove away. 'You see, my father prefers me to be a non-smoker.' On the state border he had changed into an orthodox Sikh, his father's son.

In an odd way I ceased to be an onlooker from the moment we reached Faridkot and entered the palace. I no longer felt that I was observing India, or watching David, from a seat in the wings: I was thrust onstage, there to fight my corner in the rough and tumble of palace life. It was sink or swim. Diary entries scribbled at the time tell best the way things happened.

January 27 Into Faridkot by night. Iron gates off the town street, scurry of soldiers round the car, a glimpse of peacock-blue palace above. Pulled up under a porte-cochère where we left the car and entered the building by glass doors. Confronted by a heavy rumpled figure in a rust-red cashmere sweater – His Highness. A large stone hall two storeys in height, arches everywhere, stone floor dotted with chairs. Mistakenly I grasped David's grandmother's hand and shook it warmly – it almost came off she was so surprised – while David with a practised swoop touched her feet. Beckoned by HH I sat on a comfortless cane settee between himself and this wordless granny the colour of old ivory. Is the electric rock garden hers? The instant the seat of HH's baggy trousers touched the settee a band struck up behind some archway, where it scraped away on violin and piano until bedtime. Spidery music. Rhythm brushes. Tunes you'd have heard in the Savoy dining-room in the thirties – or at David's twenty-first birthday dinner at Clay-hithe in 1959. Here is the source of his requirement to have band music playing as he ate, if a meal or an occasion was to be regarded as posh at all. Remember his penchant for the *thé dansant* at the Dorothy Café. HH had thought I was a cavalry-man (David telling him so to please him with the *idea* of my coming, regardless of consequence of lie when I arrived?) and was childishly disappointed, having looked out several books on cavalry actions for my opinion on tactics. Baulked of military talk he piled the books on my knees rather sulkily, as if I were an impostor, whilst I bowed thanks as best I could without upsetting his mother off her end of the settee. Apologising testily for the garish rugs strewn about the floor of this cavernous hall – 'just some items from my tent-camp' – he explained that the proximity of Pakistan (the border is twenty miles away) had caused him to move pictures and silver and all valuables to his houses in Delhi or Mashobra. I asked 'Don't you miss seeing your pictures, eating off silver?' Obliquely, with his rather tattered dignity, he replied simply 'Mr Glazebrook, I was brought up to a different world.'

He is a man in retreat from today's world anxious only to escape with his money. Everything he spoke of was related to money – his money and by what tricks to hang on to it in face of his enemy, the government of his own country. He doesn't listen; I think he doesn't calculate to belittle you, but achieves it without the effort of calculation – at least, towards someone as polite as I am he achieves it. Twice he apologised (once for speaking Punjabi, once for the rugs) but he is not sorry. Several times he spoke sardonically of 'your empire, Mr Glazebrook' as if was really his, not mine at all. I learned from my hour on the settee that if I was to get along I should be colder, less self-deprecatory, for he mistakes a modest attitude for servility.

At dinner (a drift of silent and unexplained figures appeared round a long table in another side-aisle of the hall) an army of soldiers do the waiting, slamming down plates, snatching up others, whilst a ferocious woman hangs about with a whisky bottle grasped in her hand. The food was full of pepper. No conversation, little talk save for stray remarks thrown out by HH: that he had liked an old secretary because 'that chap knew how to put my sense of humour into my letters'; that so-and-so 'puts sincerely or very truly yours at the bottom of his letter, but – no, no! Not a bit true!' as if, hen-like, he pecks through his letter-bag for a grain of trust. I should think few trust him, who have the choice. Perhaps because of the isolation of the throne he lacks sympathy, seems to lack fellow-feeling for what is outside himself, as though he can't imagine being a human being. In an irritable description of a road accident in the hills involving 'one of my jeeps' he emphasised that it was the jeep that was irreplaceable, not its driver. He has a passion for the army, a curious mixture of love, hate and envy. Hence the servants in battledress. Near the border as we are, many of the military men he hankers after are available to be mocked and envied. He told of a general who had asked him what might be the cost of a silver centrepiece such as the one which glittered on HH's table: 'I told him, but [fat chuckle] he didn't order one!'

By the time we returned to the draughty stone hall the entertainment was over. The band had ceased playing. Asked what time I would like to be woken in order to breakfast at half past nine, I suggested nine o'clock. Wrong reply. 'Too late!' roared out His Highness, 'bed-tea at eight for Mr Glazebrook! Goodnight Mr Glazebrook!'

I was now shown my quarters. Outside the glass door and through the arch of the porte-cochère I followed David and a muster of chatty servants across a moonlit space into a guesthouse. I seem to be alone in it. There is a high-ceilinged hall with suspended punkahs, a frayed black piano with a pot of pampas grass on it, veiled windows, assorted chests and a bridge table with cane chairs. Through one of the doors off the lobby is my room. Damp-stained walls enclosing an enormous amount of chilly space. Sparse furniture. My suitcase not unpacked, dumped in the middle of the floor. Twin beds drawn out two feet from the wall, green and cream paintwork, locked wardrobe, centre light and –summing up the gaps between planning and execution – an ancient electric fire with nowhere to plug it in. Equally ancient, and fitfully supplied with water, there is a bathroom much chipped and stained. David withdrew, with assurances that I had only to ask for whatever I wanted. I sat on one of the beds. Where could I begin to table my wants? Size, not comfort, is what counts – cubic space is the measure of grandeur. In light of this room I see why David chose the suites he did at the Khetri House hotel, and why he looked sideways when I criticised. He knew what awaited me at Faridkot – this shipwrecked ocean liner.

January 28 A feature of town life (Faridkot city is just over the wall) is the public address system available for prayers: instead of buying candles, as Christians do, here the faithful buy prayers, which are relayed through the loud-hailer between 5.30 and 7 am, reminding neighbours of your piety. Perhaps they are prayers for His Highness's health, beamed over the walls for his birthday. Wakened, I peeped through mosquito-meshed windows onto lawns and walks already swarming with servants doing nothing, fluttering along in groups, some idly sweeping the gravel. Much earlier than I had stipulated I was summoned to breakfast. In a cluster of servants I found only the old queen picking disconsolately at her fruit salad whilst trying to manage her shawls so as to keep out icy draughts from stone archways and open doors. Draughts as well as restlessness caused by servants endlessly coming and going with one piece of toast in and out across a glimpsed outdoor yard to the kitchen. The old lady – she resembles Queen Victoria, except in colour – read to herself several times a letter from Hindustani Motors, causing conversation to languish. She would not move cup or plate as much as an inch herself, waiting for large brown hands to intrude over her shawled shoulder. The number of servants has the same purpose as all the useless space in the guest-house: to enhance dignity by their presence, not to do necessary work. It is what Aksakoff describes, an unstable underclass teeming to and fro to agitate Russian country life. (Despite the crowds of them in their khaki battledress always milling about in the guest-house, my room was uncleaned today, my shoes and clothes and towels left where I dropped them.) Breakfast over, the Queen proposed a walk in the garden. I wondered if I was to be consulted about the Hindustani Motors communiqué which she brought with her. Away we trailed by stone walks and tubbed flowers. By her passing she gently, momentarily, agitated the crowd of malis into sweeping or weeding, as if a small electric shock was rippling through a somnolent hydra. There was croquet, there was tennis, and, perhaps in deference to Chief Ichalkaranji (who expresses in a book about his visit to England the opinion that 'golf is the chief pastime of the aristocracy'), there was a golf driving net; but I noticed that the mesh of the net was too large to stop a golf ball passing through it, and the croquet hoops were set so near the edge of the lawn that a game on that pitch would have been impossible, even with flamingos for mallets. The *idea* of games was what was provided; nobody wanted to play them. We wound our way between these abstract sports facilities and the small blue summerhouses dotted about the plots of grass, conversation limping along between us. A large many-trunked banyan tree crowds up against the house with the look of an octopus struggling to pull down the stricken liner. Built in 1890 and painted peacock-blue, the house has a wing added in – of all unlikely years to be adding wings to your palace – 1944. I wouldn't have been surprised by an electric rock garden somewhere about. I saw that we were circling inside a compound, and would soon regain the terrace from which we had set out.

'Do you have a rock garden, Highness?'

A gently superior smile. 'The palace garden area is amounting to almost sixteen acres all told.'

Back at the breakfast table David had appeared from whatever recesses of the tower he inhabits, and again touched Granny's feet in a businesslike though portly manner. Despite this, she knows her real place. 'Sit with me while I consume a little breakfast,' he said, taking toast from the nearest soldier and waiting for the marmalade pot to be opened for him by another. She and I sat meekly through his breakfast, Her Highness producing her Hindustani Motors document from her shawls and hesitantly asking advice about a new motor for her own establishment, David sucking down coffee and dabbing bearded lips without appearing to listen. Now, at home, he would have smoked, as he invited me to do. I wonder if he smokes secretly in his own quarters, or if he carries self-deception to the length of actually believing himself to be a non-smoker in his father's house. He rushed me to a front-door appointment with the Raja. An open US Army jeep, circa 1945, waited under the porte-cochère.

Heavy footsteps, a swirl of aides, a draught of turbulent air: HH swung through the hall, through the glass doors, into the jeep's driving seat. We were off on a tour of Faridkot, town gates opened, soldiers clinging on behind. It's a busy little town, an Asian Toytown clustered round its Diamond Jubilee clock-tower, prosperous I should think. HH proud of it. Innumerable waves of the royal hand to indicate landmarks or good works: 'my second guest-house, my girls' school, my racecourse, my hospital, my aerodrome'. Buildings which had somehow become heaps of stone were passed by without comment. Earthquake? Enemy action? Punishment? Any speculation was feasible. We finished up doing a lap of honour in 'my sport stadium' with HH standing at the wheel to acknowledge the imaginary cheers of a people for its triumphant raja, hands clasped overhead in a full-blooded humorous way which is attractive because it's a shade rueful. He is a grey-bearded, bushy figure, rumbustious as stout men are, strands of hair escaping from turban and beard-net. Planted throughout the town are the extravagant gestures of his ancestors, and he knows all too well what the clocktowers and public halls and statues under canopies had cost. Money and taxes. Bored of money and taxes I said 'The pity is that one should have to worry about money all the time.' 'I don't worry myself, Mr Glazebrook,' he retorted, 'my accountant is paid a very princely sum to worry for me.' We came shortly to 'my stables'. Sorry-looking police horses in stalls – 'I maintain only a very few nags now' – then into barns containing a bizarre armoury of relics from World War II. More US jeeps ('I bought up 164 of them in '44'), two armoured personnel carriers, an amphibious Weasel and an old field-gun. Which part of his mind did such hardware comfort? Was the Weasel for crossing the Sutlej into Pakistan at the head of his servant-army? Or for self-defence, a fighting retreat into the hills, where his treasure was already stored? Lap of victory in the sports stadium, or bolt for cover to Mashobra? I thought of David's wild-eyed uncle striding round the table with his mind harried into confusion by the massacres of Independence.

That immediate collapse of North India into disorder in 1947 had shaken the princes' confidence forever – rather the way the Mutiny had shaken British confidence, as much in themselves as in the Indians they governed – and David's father evidently comforted himself against that latent fear with the *matériel* of mobilisation stored in his garage.

Back in the palace garden a line of chairs had been set out, an outdoor bar erected at a discreet distance, the old queen summoned, and there we sat drinking beer in a row, listening to favourites from old musicals – *Tip Toes, Lady Be Good, Salad Days* – tinkling out of the ballroom windows which our chairs faced. Hoopoes hopped about on the grass. After a desultory interval we all four crowded into a small marble summerhouse, its outside surfaces intricately decorated with carvings, where lunch was expected. There was just room at the table for a newcomer led our way across the lawns by servants, a small neat figure in a nautch coat who had come to stay, his white walrus moustache a bold feature, in his eyes the uncertain look of bewilderment which accompanies deafness. On and on we waited, an icy wind whistling through the pavilion's lattices, till HH's military 'pal' was announced. I did not think the space would hold this tall fierce Sikh, let alone his ADC, luckily a tiny man who sat next me, legs swinging, and talked about cricket in a low voice, ready and waiting to be interrupted by a comment or a question from his superior. The Army (and I seem to have met a lot of Army men) is the most Anglophile, even Anglomanic, institution left in India; strange that the blood-stained instrument of oppression and imperialism, pilloried on those Republic Days floats, should be so eagerly copied. When I said so he agreed, evidently assuming that I despised 'politicals' and applauded the Army.

In the afternoon His Highness and David and I went out partridge-shooting.

Taking a jeep armed with a .303 rifle, a .22, a pistol and a .410 shotgun, we drove out of town into the country. Areas of desert, patches of jungle grass fifteen feet high; fields of green wheat, some of them waterlogged; an extensive forest of sheesham, spindly trees fifteen years old, all leaning one way. Flat country once desert. We bucketed across it on sandy tracks. At an army encampment in quasi-desert HH saluted the guard smartly, ever hankering for the military life, and explained who he was as a *laissez-passer* across his kingdom ('I am His Highness the Raja and this is the Tikka Sahib and an English gentleman – we are shooting a few partridges for the pot') before driving on. Even desert and scrub jungle produce people, some on foot, some on camel-back or bicycle, others cutting firewood, a population giving the impression of patient journeying and patient toil. When the fancy takes him to question a peasant the Raja stops the jeep not beside the man but ten or so yards off, so that the man must run humbly after him to reply. Then HH drives on without a word of thanks. To an English eye it looks arrogant and unmannerly, but a foreigner is no judge of customs.

English as it sounded, our partridge-shooting was very unEnglish in its execution. The plan was to drive along a track until a covey was spied, then to blaze away with rifle, pistol and shotgun as the birds sat tight or scampered for safety. 'I shoot only for the pot,' HH explained as he reloaded a heavy army pistol after a fruitless barrage. The covey had scurried unharmed into the jungle, and I asked if we shouldn't follow on foot to flush them for a shot flying. They looked surprised. 'Take a good few shells,' advised the Raja, 'take care where you are putting your feet in the bush, Mr Glazebrook.' He gave orders over his shoulder in Punjabi to the thin-shanked menial in the back who climbed down from the jeep with sighs of peevish reluctance for this martyrdom, banging his staff bitterly on the ground and shaking his head. 'My farm manager will go with you, Mr Glazebrook. Good luck.' We set off. Almost immediately we were screened from the track and isolated in tall jungle-grass over our heads. It was bone-dry, silent; just the hiss when we touched the white fronds. I advanced with the .410 at the ready, the farm manager tarrying in my footsteps and prodding the ground with his staff. He had done little beating for partridges and wasn't keen. The deeper we went into the jungle the deeper grew the silence. I wondered about snakes and scorpions and other pests. I led my party cautiously in a semi-circle and out again onto the track.

Proceeding in the jeep we shot nothing, then had tea. A fitted wicker basket, thermos and cups from the early days of plastic, egg sandwiches. HH talked of the 'sport' we had so far enjoyed just as if we had shot a cartful in Lincolnshire. When I asked 'Do you fish, Highness?', he replied complacently 'I will show you my rods.' After tea I was sent off into the field with the .410 to shoot 'another few brace', HH's warning ringing in my ears that he only liked his birds 'shot dead, through the neck please'.

Shooting over, we stopped at the 'home farm' to drop off the manager. A deserted dust compound, mud-walled, a tethered nag, the bump and squeak of a well-pump the only sound. Desolation at the end of the world. The Indian penchant for describing things by English names – partridge-shooting, home farm – leads an Englishman to expect what is familiar only to feel derisive when it is not.

Back to the palace in cold evening dark to find new arrivals formed up on hard chairs in the guest-house lobby. Beside the walrus-moustached ancient from lunch sat a biscuit-maker from Simla, a Mr Worra; next to him a tall anxious Sikh with a furrowed brow; then a mild bespectacled Sikh (who had been David's tutor) with a wife wrapped in a donkey-jacket. A little bewildered by so much company I took a chair in their circle. It was a signal for there to begin one of the deep silences of India under the flicker and drizzle of yellow light from an imperfectly wired chandelier over our heads.

Bridge before dinner, played with an ancient pack which HH occasionally has washed. He and his mother versus the biscuit-maker and me. We sat down at a worn-out baize table set so near the glass entrance-door that no one could come in or go out unless I stood up. Usual freezing palace draughts. The old queen's predatory hands clawed up the pasteboards, HH talked over his shoulder to the frowning Sikh and to a tiny black pilot, almost a midget, who had both drawn up chairs behind him – and Worra, with the loose lip and vacant eye of an obsessive, flicking out cards at top speed, scratching the made tricks towards him across the table, playing only a few cards before chucking the rest of his hand on the table with a rattle of Hindi. I never enjoyed cards less.

Dinner for a large company, twenty or more, gathered round a teakwood table. The unseen band played through its arch, the servants swarmed, the guests were silent. David and I, sitting far apart, tried to keep a ball, any ball, crossing the net: 'David, are there ancient houses and antique furniture in everyday use in India?' 'I wonder, Philip. I don't think the Moghuls did much sitting about the place on chairs, did they?' No one listened, no one spoke except HH shouting out 'What?' down the table so rudely that I shut up too and the whole table sat in rebarbative silence whilst the band played hits from the *Titanic*'s repertoire.

Bridge after dinner was hellish. Wearing a woollen hat against the cold the biscuit-maker criticised my play either in English I couldn't understand or in Hindi addressed to Their Highnesses, whilst himself overbidding so grossly that we went down 450 points in three rubbers. It pleased me more to see him reluctantly fishing money out of his purse than it annoyed me to lose myself. Nevertheless, annoyance made me speak sharply and laconically to Worra and to HH too. They didn't care a fig: the card-table code in India allows a lot of scrapping before umbrage is taken. We played only for 50 paise a hundred, the low stakes due to a rash moment in the old queen's past when she got into a bridge school led by the Faridkot dentist who took 2,000 rupees off her in a week. David told me this, walking me across to the guest-house by moonlight, his inquiries ever solicitous of my comfort and happiness. In face of his formal inquiries I somehow didn't like to point out to him the uncleaned state of my room, the shoes with the trees pushed into them upside down, the clothes I'd gone shooting in still chucked on the bed, the unemptied ashtrays. My dear fellow (he might have replied) there are servants, therefore surely the work is done: worry yourself with no further inquiries.

January 29 Woken by ragged gunfire celebrating the Raja's birthday. Muzzle-loaders on the lawn, wheezy bagpipes quavering away as the smoke of the salute cleared. Breakfast amid the tramp of servants, then a wait to catch HH and wish him happy birthday and give him my present, a cashmere jersey which he held momentarily, like a bishop blessing a baby, before discarding it to an aide and bustling on with his crowd of attendants half-running behind them. Then I took my place in a row of hard chairs facing the house across scraps of lawn while the pipe band marched about the garden playing Highland airs. New faces abounded, men in skimpy suits and worn shoes, all of them fluttering their hands in namaste as the jolly Raja strode by. David's cousin Michael (who inherits everything if David dies before his father) is a sly, insinuating creature of thirty-odd who irritated me by saying in my ear that he's never seen the garden so shabby, and irritated me further by telling me *á propos de bottes* that he had no need to work. Black Michael of Ruritania came into my head. But on his sister Wendy, whom I'd met in Delhi and who lives in New York, I fell as if upon a friend from childhood, or at least from some nearly forgotten pre-Faridkot era of my life, when I lived at ease in another reality. We talked: silence is the threat, ice ever ready to form over the pool if you stop splashing for a moment.

My neighbour at lunch was David's shy mild tutor who whispered away much to my interest about Indian universities, the language problems caused by the three tongues, Urdu, Hindi and Punjabi. Few others talked; they keep their eyes on their platters, too, so that effort is needed to attract their attention.

Back to the bridge table after lunch.

Table and chairs set outdoors under an umbrella where last night's four gathered and sat down amid a crowd of watchers. As he dealt the first hand HH said in his rumbustious manner that all through the game yesterday they had discussed my play in Hindi and had concluded that a rich Englishman had fallen into their hands whom it was their duty to fleece. He has that irritating ability (an attribute of power?) to make you forgive his rudeness the moment he says a pleasant word to you or takes your arm. About poor old Worra being puzzled by my bidding, HH said 'We subject people are always trying to make out what the lordly English are thinking, isn't it so, Highness?' (he calls his mother Highness). Catching me noticing that he appeared to have taken a quick squint at Worra's cards he growled out very comically, 'Oh, horrible natives! – they are peeping in each other's hands.' Today I played reasonably and twice successfully doubled Their Highnesses.

Next after bridge on our busy agenda came a visit with David's uncle (plus his children Black Michael and Wendy) in jeeps crowded with ADCs to the uncle's house (he farms) where the stud (plain old grey stallion) was pulled out of his stable to be admired. Mud walls, and dust spiralling off the enclosures into a landscape as flat as a dish. On, raising more dust, to the 'stud farm', a range of barns like a mud-bank pierced with holes like the nests of enormous swallows, each hole with a stake tied across it for a door, behind the doors the mares and yearlings. Boys led out the animals whilst the stud groom flooded me with Hindi. Not hard to pick on the better made ones, but David's uncle was surprised and a little gratified that I knew one end of a horse from the other. Michael on the other hand was ratty, claiming that one moth-eaten animal was 'the finest colt in India', which led David (who knows not one thing about horses) to speak of grander studs he was familiar with elsewhere, rather belittling the establishment of his cousins. Indian ways with the sport of kings are devious: for instance, the foal of a mare covered by an army remount stallion (a popular but illegal union) is given the official pedigree 'breeding unknown'. It only fools the outsider, who is puzzled by the number of winners coming in at startlingly short odds with this unpromising pedigree.

What do Black Michael and Wendy, the dispossessed cousins, think of David and his complacency? David's death would make Michael heir to Faridkot. They are standing on ground soaked with the blood of family murders, committed in attempts to reach the throne. And Wendy? Slight, boneless, honey-voiced, vivacious in the sense that she laughs a lot; but discontent haunts her face. Her style is to belittle everything Indian, say she is bored, wish she was back in New York. And in New York? Spins tales of her uncle the fabled raja and his glittering court, I shouldn't wonder. She too would be nearer the throne if David perished. Still, I believe she is the old queen's favourite, so that attention in that direction may secure an inheritance of sorts without recourse to knife-box or poison cabinet.

Bridge, the customary four, in the entrance-hall before dinner. Interesting to see the large many-arched space become enriched and animated with knots of turbans and wagging beards – peopled as it should be, buzzing with voices, emptiness filled as chairs were pushed into groups and occupied – a reception hall fulfilling its purpose, the Raja with his bridge-slaves and his toadies the suitably idiosyncratic touch by the door. Reflectively, half to himself as he watched his guests, in his deep humorous voice the Raja muttered 'In Faridkot also they wash behind their ears when you ask them to dine!' The observation made him laugh. ''Tis merry in hall when beards wag all.' Then he gathered up his cards and the game continued.

Dinner. Sat next to the old queen again – where I suppose precedence would seat me until one or other of us died – and toiled up the rockfaces of many subjects trying to drag Her Highness after me. No depth of hold achieved in any. If I say 'Did you have a town house in Lahore? When did you used to go there? What was it like?' she wears her sibylline smile and replies quietly 'We maintained four houses in Lahore.' Next question please. They will none of them talk about the 1947 Partition riots, as though it was a servants' brawl no gentlefolk witnessed, and to a question about that subject she says nothing at all, working her bony hands under the table. In youth she lived in purdah, and watched life through lattices; perhaps explaining why she is now like an ancient sixteen-year-old. Bending her head slightly in my direction she told me in confidence, to justify some shortcoming in the meal, that the cook had suffered a bout of 'paralysis' that evening. I nodded wisely. The Raja (whose voice always silenced the table, stamping out any little shoots of talk which might have sprung up elsewhere) told of a Highland hotel on the Oykel where the management, ashamed of having no private bathroom to offer, wrote 'His Highness Only' on the door of the one public bathroom. 'Very kind man.' He spoke with emphasis and satisfaction of this signal recognition of his standing, even in the wastes of Sutherland. I thought of Queen Victoria travelling incognito amongst the inns of Northern Scotland, and it seemed almost as if the two royal parties might have bumped into each other, at the inn-door at Lairg perhaps, where the innkeeper would have cudgelled his brains vainly as to what to write on his bathroom door. If the old queen resembles Queen Victoria, her son is a little like Edward VII, the rumbling arbitrary laugh, the unpredictable royal humour. Hard to know when he is laughing at you and when at himself, for he is above all a creature of rapid whims. David too: in his father's impenetrable style he related how he had arrived at some English house to find a flag flying from its roof, the host explaining that they invariably flew a flag when royalty was staying. 'I told them I was only ex-royalty,' David said. Self-mockery or not? Now that I know a little of his father, a little of India, I am inclined rather ruefully to see in David a self-awareness and self-mockery which I hadn't taken into account before. What terms were he and his father on? I could not imagine them informally together. Would they talk Hindi, or Punjabi; or (like the Tsarist nobility speaking French amongst themselves) would English be the language they chose in private? No use asking David; he would catch the drift of my question and answer 'Hindi of course' rather than answering truthfully.

Bridge after dinner. Beginning to find my feet with the biscuit-maker for partner: we ended 340 points up. I told him as he bubbled and fumed at me over some shortcoming, 'I find it very difficult to follow you when you get excited. Calm down, Mr Worra.' HH laughed, but care is essential; no king likes his fool teased by outsiders.

Escorting me across to the guest-house when play closed – he had long disappeared from the hall and must have left orders to be fetched so that he could perform this hospitable courtesy – David said, in talking of games, that he expects to beat anyone he meets in England at any of the games he is prepared to play. 'In India not so; opponents need picking with care.' And yet he is, or seems to be, a good loser...or perhaps he let me win, just that once, at chess, like a hound allowed a lick of the fox's blood to keep him keen on the chase.

January 30 After a lengthy breakfast at which the biscuit-maker (woolly hat in place) made himself marmalade sandwiches while the walrus puffed and mumbled (tooth trouble behind that moustache?), the old queen rather touchingly followed me into the ballroom where she shyly suggested 'a wander in the garden'. Is it etiquette that she cannot stroll alone? She has nothing to say, nothing she wants to discuss as we wander; but I daresay the spectacle of a solitary walker is thought pitiable amongst the faintly hostile crowds of idle servants. Hence the flurry of ADCs at whose centre HH hurries through life. Hence the background of 'company' David made sure of, in his lodgings or his college at Cambridge, for turban-winding duties or more commonly just for (deferential) presences whilst he sipped Johnnie Walker and tapped his foot to rumbas on his gramophone.

In a jeep packed with hangers-on, personal flag fluttering, HH and David and I dashed through the streets to the Durbar Hall in the fort for the Baba Farid Convention.

I was escorted into the Hall by a quiet old gentleman who praised with clasped hands HH's administration of the State. Not a village where he couldn't call men by name, not a road built that he wasn't out morning and evening at the site. As an engineer? No. As a strong man with a pickaxe? No. Just as the princely presence, the encourager, the inspirer; the position he was born to (David too) and has fulfilled well, but a position in which the ignorant and jealous think they could put any stooge they might like to replace him with. What would the village people think of him (or David) if he took off his shirt and worked beside them on the road? They wouldn't like it. Tolstoy doesn't give us the thoughts of the peasants when Levin, for his own reasons, descends among them to ply his scythe with theirs, but I guess it lowered his prestige, except in his own eyes. I guess the only way HH would be welcomed into their depths by his villagers would be if he had come down to fight beside them, like the last of the Ottonian sultans at the fall of Constantinople, to seek with them an anonymous death against a common enemy. The old queen, when I asked her on our morning walk if she ever gardened herself, smiled sweetly and thought it unnecessary to reply.

There sat the dispossessed Raja in his erstwhile Durbar Hall amongst ferret-eyed politicians and a rabble of humbler men – waiting, waiting, waiting for the Minister to arrive. How patient they all are, I said to HH. All are hoping for some favour, he replied, and would not give up their place or their chance if they must wait for the bigwig till the crack of doom. Had he thought of seeking political power himself, I asked, as many ex-rulers had done, turning their subjects' loyalty into votes? 'Mr Glazebrook, I would rather sweep a crossing' – the disdainful anachronism, horse-drawn London referred to by a Victorian country magnate. The chairs we sat on bore the British royal cipher, having been made for Queen Victoria who rejected them. Do I believe this? Does he, as he tells me? His Durbar Hall is a lordly, lofty chamber with a good plaster cornice and empty chains where chandeliers had hung before removal to safety in the hills. There is something a little faint-hearted about the removal of so much clobber to Mashobra, which seems unworthy of a fighting Punjab chief. Still, he keeps a field-gun in his garage.

When the Minister at last arrived (one and a half hours late) he was a little parched stick of a man, papery and bored, snootier far in his greeting and looking on than the hearty Raja. Now was the time for speech and song. It was like a school prize-giving, or a gathering to cheer on the village talent. It was fearfully dull. Everyone who can read (as well, no doubt, as those who claim they can) wears spectacles, so that the glitter of glass under snowy turbans on the dais, as the learned inclined towards each other for consultation, gave off flashes like an electrical storm. At the centre sat the Minister sunk in thought or boredom. He, with plums to distribute, had no need to be polite. HH showed irritation only when at last we were leaving and found the ministerial car hogging the porte-cochère like a pig asleep across his doorway. 'Even my own porch blocked,' he said, walking angrily out of the shade to his jeep waiting in the sun with its soldier-driver.

Bridge from five o'clock till 8.45 as guests arrived and the band played. Though the game went my way I was irritable and left crossly to change for dinner. David, ever watchful, came to my room. Still angry, I chose the servants to be angry about – my room filthy, heaps of damp towels, shoes uncleaned, nothing touched for two days except that a pack of cigarettes had been stolen. Looking stiffly round he said 'No valeting I see.' I said I didn't want valeting, I wanted the room put straight and a two-day-old coffee cup removing. You have to put up silently with ill usage by your host, but of his servants' ill usage you can complain.

Another long dinner next the old queen. As usual the dim gent on her other side never spoke – kept his eyes on his plate –

and as usual my own voice and David's and his father's were the only voices raised. Her Highness never asks me a question about anything, either general or personal, accepting my presence as if I'd dropped from the sky into the seat at her side. I have dug deep in the conversational barrel to prevent her slipping away from me into silence and oblivion like the Cheshire Cat. Asked if she'd ever been yachting she replied 'His Highness was always maintaining a yacht on the Sutlej before.' 'Before!' – the very word was like a bell. Everything that mattered was 'before'. In answer to some other question she told me with pleasure and almost with energy of the ruin of the Raja of Jeen: 'He is selling everything.' 'Do you not like him, Highness?' Faintly again: 'Oh, he is quite nice.' It is the *frisson* of gossip, scandal, blood in the water, that gives her malice a moment's pleasure. 'I may try to buy one of his clocks,' she whispered. Down goes the raja, and she snaps up a clock left floating where the sharks got him. David, keeping just on its legs the illusion that conversation was general by addressing me across intervening silent guests, asked for my 'first impressions of India'. But he insists that I have certain impressions – relief that Delhi is much less dusty than I expected, for instance – so that the conversation is not a discussion. He had programmed me – careful to have shown me only the safe India of Delhi and Agra; now he pushed the button for a safe print-out.

At a dinner party in Delhi one night the general talk had turned on snakes. The Belgian ambassador told us that he had found a hill-snake in his sitting-room one day, whereupon David asserted, and tried to persuade us, that His Excellency had made an error common with foreigners (anxious for exotica to put into postcards home) and had mistaken the harmless earthworm for the snake which he expected India to provide. According to David there were really no snakes to speak of in India, they existed in the wishful thinking of visitors. Now I had read in an Indian paper a day or two earlier that 10,000 people are killed by snake-bite in India each year. But when I put forward this figure it was immediately challenged as absurdly high by some, absurdly low by others; until I wasn't sure myself whether the paper's figure had been 1,000 or 10,000 or 100,000. Amongst the exaggerated statistics of India any figure seems both possible and improbable. David took the confusion of the snake-party as proof of his contention that there are no snakes worth troubling about in India. I looked at him. Did anyone else at the dinner party know what I knew, that this poo-pooher of snakes never took his customary walk in the Lodi gardens without first arming himself with his sword-stick in case he encountered amongst the tombs the 'Lodi cobra' of which he spoke with reverence and alarm?

The Indian mind is hard to contend with. After a week or two of Rajmahal dinners I'd end up offering the expected printout, agreeing that Delhi was much less dusty than I had expected. I'd be subdued, as I expect both HH and his son long to see an Englishman subdued, by the practices of an Indian court. Talking of Freemasonry (from an English mason I had learned that he is a Grand Master) the Raja said with a glint of malice that it was 'the only way we could get near enough to speak to Mr Glazebrook's ancestors'. It preys on his mind. He has caused a book to be insinuated into my bedroom – I'm sure his hand is behind its appearance there – which details the catastrophe that overtook the British (due to age and incompetence in the high command) when an entire Britsh army was massacred during its retreat from Kabul to Jalalabad in the First Afghan War in 1842. I had no idea our behaviour was so shameful, so craven, or that the disaster was so complete. HH has caused me to inform myself of humiliating facts, as he intended. 'Leave him amongst his dirty ashtrays and his uncleaned shoes, but make sure he knows the facts of the First Afghan War.' Such may well have been his orders.

Yet I like him. In his entrance-hall after dinner he positively danced to avoid the two-handed swoop made towards his feet by a ten-year-old boy who had dined at Rajmahal. 'No, no! It is custom of another generation and I don't want you doing it!' If you penetrate no deeper than the ornamental shell – foot-touching, band scraping away behind the arras, six greybeards armed with .303s at the door, a bugler, every booted foot crashing to attention whenever HH is glimpsed – if you look no further it is all rather ridiculous. But the remote past is close at hand in India; only a century and a half ago it was still the Middle Ages, a court gathered round a fighting chief. Dwellers in these native states have had 150 years to rid themselves of habits of mind and social conditions shaken off in Europe at the end of the fifteenth century.

Bridge till 12.15 am: none of them care that I don't like playing with them. They don't notice an uncongenial atmosphere. When Worra quibbled about overtricks HH hissed out 'Biscuit-maker!' with his boiling-kettle laugh. There is something of the bully in him which finds satisfaction in creating an unhappy state of mind in those around him. He is rough and gentle by turns. Having shouted through the archway at the band all evening ('Too loud, Susa, too loud') he dismisses them about midnight with a last great shout: 'Goodnight, Susa; take a jeep, don't walk': fiddle ceases behind arch, scraping of chairs, mice feet patter away, silence.

David, coming again to my room to assuage ruffled feathers, confirmed my opinion of his cousin Black Michael. Sly, incompetent, vainglorious and resentful. He married a 'town girl' from Faridkot, failed at three jobs (one of them tea-planting), sponged off the old queen until he was so ill-mannered she threw him out, now lives at his father's farm reading for his MA (*aetat.* 30) without money enough for independence. How he must hope for the heart attack or the car accident which, in this century, has replaced the assassin's knife as means of reaching a Punjab throne. David, the luck of the draw on his side, can condescend to all his relations. So long as he is careful how he drives.

January 31 Breakfast beside Mr Worra. He did not speak, communicating with himself by eructation. Every day the same threadbare brown suit, same grubby shirt, greasy tie. HH strode magnificently into our breakfast-room, his great slope-shouldered bulk wrapped in a dressing-gown, silvery locks loosely twisted up without a turban, his hands carrying before him an enormous biscuit tin into which he delved, chuckling, to distribute to his guests as if to dogs the fruit of Mr Worra's labours. Teasing, bullying: a fine line divides them, the difference in an autocrat's moods. He enters, waves a hand: 'Sit, please sit. Ah, my dear, how are you? Yes, yes, he is a very – nice – man [emphasising and separating the words]. Mr Glazebrook, how did you sleep? That is a very – good –suit you are wearing. How are you?' Charmed is how I am: bullied and teased and charmed. When he had swept off, leaving behind him the rumour that HH of Bharatpur had shot his brother-in-law, David said 'I don't believe that. The people that Papa keeps around him are vying with each other in agreeing with him, and if he says HH of Bharatpur is mad they all try to make up better stories to prove it is true.' His father tries to do away with the foot-touching: will David, when his turn comes, try to do away with the toadies?

On the road to Chandigarh – David and Wendy and I were as jolly in the car as three children let out of school – I happened to say, à propos the Kabul disaster, that it was surprising that a race capable of such mismanagement ever did conquer India. David, eyes on the road ahead as he drove, said 'Rather like your bridge. First day, rumours were flying round the place that Mr Glazebrook couldn't play for toffee. Then by next day people were sort of saying actually he's rather good, only he doesn't play our way.'

There was, after all, a Second Afghan War, which the British won.

Seven

A few days later I flew on my own to Madras. 'Where should I stay in Madras, Highness?' I had asked David's father. 'Go to the Connemara,' he replied with decision. I had done so, my taxi from the airport immediately surrounded by hotel servants darting hither and thither like a swarm of bees, my luggage grabbed, myself shuttled along the hotel's colonnaded veranda, which was lined with high-backed planters' chairs under slowly-turning punkahs, into a reception hall dimmed but hardly cooled by excluding the light of day. I could see why it suited HH: the confusion of many servants, the empty spaces, the decayed lordliness of it all; it might have been copied from his own palace.

At dinner, too, the band had played just as it had played at Rajmahal; only here, in the heat, as an accompaniment to music, the glasses on each table rattled together to the vibrations of the air-conditioning plant which shook the hotel like a liner's engines. The Connemara was an extension of His Highness's idea of reality, and of David's too. Accustomed to living with them I felt comfortable in it. If this was 'South India' I was reassured at the prospect of my weeks alone. I dined, idled on the veranda, returned to my room to write letters; and there, ready for me on the carpet when I switched on the light, waited an enormous brilliantly-coloured centipede. It looked dangerous. It waited in enigmatic stillness for a decision. I couldn't name it, or classify it, or in any way lift it out of my life with the tongs of science. I couldn't physically put it out of the window because air-conditioning meant the windows were sealed shut. I could ignore it, or I could kill it. David's scrupulous care in North India had protected me from insects and bugs. I remembered the way he had argued snakes out of existence; and remembered also that he carried a sword-stick in case his argument was fallacious. I gave the creature a wide berth and sat at the writing table, aware of its eyes on my back. I couldn't ignore it because I knew that it would disappear from view, and I would then have no idea where it had chosen next to lie in wait. Too uncomfortable to write, I turned to face the problem, the first problem David couldn't solve for me.

I had seen North India through eyes which David had put into my head by the thoroughness of his hospitality. Arrived back in Delhi from Faridkot we had knocked up Massih and the Mug, and received their welcome, and eaten the scratch dinner they put together quite as if it was as much my home-coming as David's. After a few days he drove me to the airport, courteous to the last, and returned himself to the life he had generously shared with me, while my plane waited to take me to the South. As it started to taxi towards the runway a lone dog, asleep in the shadow of a wing, got on his three legs, shook his torn coat and trotted off to find another scrap of shade in which to nap. There was something enviable, I didn't quite know what, in such cheery independence. India looks after her own. My plane climbed through the circling vultures and droned south. The hills below were reduced to mud-ripples in a dried up puddle, the villages to hubs of cartwheels whose spokes were tracks raying out into desert or jungle. I wondered what it was like down there, in such remoteness as the shadow of our plane crossed. What lay ahead? I had asked David how I should best get from Madras to Pondicherry, my first objective, and he had replied 'Taxi' (with the brusque disinterest he deployed against all mention of my coming journey in the South) so that I had asked the driver who took me from the air-port to the Connemara if he would drive me to Pondicherry next day, and what he would charge me for the journey. David's father had told me that people in the South would roll their heads from side to side when they meant to say yes, so I was prepared for that. The taxi lurched, the driver gesticulated, vast sums of rupees were mentioned by him and mocked by me. Then with his sudden capitulation – 'As you like, master, you pay what you think good' – came the sensation of stepping on air where the next step should have been, together with the discreditable feeling of bargaining with the poor. Taxi booked, a path of sorts extended the realities of North India into the unknown South.

Poverty, and how I would feel about it, was one of the factors to be faced in the South. With David I had beaten down what I felt to be bourgeois English hand-wringing at the beggars' stumps pushed into my face, and had adopted David's stout indifference. I ignored the clamour. Once in Delhi a shoeshine boy had darted out of his hiding-place like a snake from its hole and dabbled a fingerful of polish onto one of my toecaps. According to him, it was a capture. He followed me down the street, dabbing at my other shoe like a brave determined to bring down his bison with a second arrow. I tried to ignore him, half-hopping, half-running to escape his grasping hands and his cries for payment for polish already expended. Trying to ignore the poor never seemed to go quite smoothly for me as it did for David. Nevertheless I was resolved. I would not let my heart go out painfully to the lame and injured, whether animal or human. I would be irritated by them, as Indians appeared to be. India was all of a piece, and must be taken together or let alone. I remembered what Nirad Chaudhuri had written: 'A man who cannot endure dirt, dust, stench, noise, ugliness, disorder, heat and cold, has no right to live in India. I would say that no man is a fit citizen of India until he has conquered squeamishness to the point of being indifferent to the presence of fifty lepers in various stages of decomposition within a hundred yards, or not minding the sight of human excreta everywhere, even in a big city.'

Determined to be fit for India in Chaudhuri's sense, I began by taking off my shoe and smashing the beautiful centipede to pieces with it, trying to pretend to myself that it was the easy, automatic reaction of an old India hand when the noxious native fauna had penetrated his defences.

By taxi, according to David's instructions, I reached Pondicherry next evening. All day, driving the 100-odd miles down the coast of Coromandel, the driver had stopped where he liked. Sometimes the place had appealed to me, sometimes it hadn't; in any case I had been able to say 'Drive on.' In this way we had visited the Madras Art Gallery, Fort St George – of which I remember nothing – and the headquarters of the Theosophical Society, whose sinister quiescence I clearly recall. Just as I thought we were settled for the run south the taxi driver turned off the road onto a wide driveway which led us to the colonnaded portico of Mrs Besant's Society. It was an overbearing place: I felt unprepared in a way that was uncomfortable. There was silence, unusual outdoors in India, odd enough to make you look round apprehensively for its cause. White guest-houses were grouped round the main building, dusty walks led away among trees and flowers. The heat was very still. In niches round a pavement of marble stood statues of religious leaders, above them, emblazoned on the pediment, were carved the words 'No Religion Is Higher than Truth'. Then, hardly disturbing the silence more than a wisp of smoke would have done, there rose from the temple a querulous monologue in English, a lady's voice quavering up faint and thin, infinitely tired but infinitely determined, an imprisoned voice complaining or praying out of an inexhaustible store of resentment and distress. When I thought of my own destination – the ashram of Sri Aurobindo, now in the hands of The Mother – that immured voice alarmed me. I climbed back into my taxi and signalled to the driver to take me away.

All day I'd been able to have myself driven away from what I didn't want to explore, or lacked courage to investigate – that's the beauty of a taxi – but when we drove into Pondicherry (my taxi driver careful to avoid the fish laid out to dry on the road

[92]

into town) I knew I had reached the end of the taxi ride, the end of skipping what I didn't fancy, the end of the road laid out for me by others. Here I must stay. Here I must find out for myself how to live. I looked out with caution at the town that was to surround me, if not to immure me, for an indefinite period. People had called in here for lunch and stayed for ever.

What I saw through the taxi window was not India but provincial France. Clean house-fronts with French-grey shutters faced the street, their numbers in white on blue plaques; in the squares the statues struck Gallic attitudes under leafless trees; there was a dusting of the litter of India on top – men stretched out asleep on the pavement, pan-stalls, handcarts of smoking nuts – just the surface dressing of India scattered over seedy Mediterranean France. Through these streets my driver asked his way to 10 rue Suffren, the ashram guest-house into which I had booked myself from England, and all too soon the taxi stopped before a pair of high sun-faded wooden doors. I paid him and got out. My baggage was put out beside me. With the disappearing taxi David's control over my life faded like a weakening radio signal, and I was left alone in front of formidable doors.

In the doors I discovered a wicket, which I stepped through with my luggage. I was in a courtyard, large pots of jungle greenery standing on its cobbles, marigolds, a scatter of empty chairs on a veranda facing me below a tall French house. A girl appeared drying her hands on her apron, showed me through a louvred door off the courtyard into a half-dark room, and left me. The stone floor and its height made it cool, the closed green shutters made it dark. Two wooden bedframes had corner posts for mosquito nets. There was a table and chair, and a tiny wardrobe. Behind a screen was a cold shower and basin and lavatory. I might have arrived at a dubious hotel a few miles from the southern Rhône. I did not unpack, but reserved judgement. Supper was eaten to solemn music in the company (at separate tables) of an English couple, two Italian women and another, single, woman of indeterminate race. Mosquitoes drilled holes in my ankles. When I had eaten a little I went back to my room and sat on the bed considering my position. Did I need or want all this peace and quiet? What would I do with it? The fact of the wardrobe being far too small to hold my clothes seemed significant. I remembered my feelings fifteen years earlier when I had arrived one September evening at Perugia and found myself faced with entering an institution, the Università degli Stranieri.

My plan then had been to learn Italian to fit myself out for the post promised me of attaché to the Rome embassy. I was twenty-two, had left Cambridge in June, and my freedom rebelled against the unwelcome feeling of being reabsorbed into communal life, student circles, shades of the prison house which threatened even as I stood at notice boards and searched for my hostel. After an enchanting September on the coast of Argentario I felt an individuality, a newness of life, which my first glimpses of Perugia already threatened. But what else could I do, how else learn Italian to continue my plan? I leaned on a balustrade in the upper town gazing out over the view in the last of the sun and wondered what to decide. On a hillside a few miles off the evening light glowed on a little town, a handful of white stones. I put my luggage back in the car, descended the twisting road from Perugia, sped across the plain and climbed to that town, its candour now turned all to rose by the setting sun. It was Assisi. I took lodgings and stayed till Christmas, living alone, learning Italian, and (for the first time in my life) writing a book.

Dodging Perugia may have turned out right or wrong, but I have always recognised that what made me do it was want of determination in face of initial dismay. Assisi was a retreat. The same dismay inclined me against joining the circle I had seen at its supper in rue Suffren; but where was I to run to from Pondicherry? No Assisi offered sanctuary. I hadn't the happy self-reliance of the dog at the airport, which could shift from the shade of one airliner to another.

Eight

I had not sat pondering very long on my bed in that oubliette of a room before Mr Goyle, fragment of the Universal Mind, came stealing in. He was the manager of the establishment. Neat of hair, earnest, short, with a mild glow of conviction lighting up his eyes behind his spectacles, he managed far more than the mere outward needs of his guests, food and rest, for he was tuned to another wavelength, a prison governor listening to his captives' inmost secrets by means of bugged cells, and in consequence he moved about the house guided and informed by whispers of the Higher Wisdom in his ear. He wore a white shirt and a dhoti, and a rare smile showed brown teeth. What you noticed at once about his presence was the calm: it was like a sedative, and he went round the rooms under his care issuing himself in opiate form to excitable guests. I noticed too, as he glided about, that his hands were very large in proportion to his body, like the Buddha's. We talked, friends at once. He knew the hesitation of my nature, the uncertainty of my mind. No doubt they were commonplace in beached wanderers found on the ashram's shore.

This ashram, once the court of Sri Aurobindo and now that of the Mother, was the central point of the universe. I had arrived. He nodded when I named the friend who had roused my curiosity about the place and caused me to make it an objective in my Indian travels: like everything else that happened, it was just as he had expected. My friend's wife had regretted not staying till I came, he said. But I'd never met her, I objected. He raised those large hands: meetings of the mind were what counted. She would be back before I left, bringing her children, settling down to perfect peace. But my friend was her husband, I told him, and what was he supposed to make of his wife moving to South India with his children? Again the beatific hand waved like a lotus leaf to nullify criticism. I understood that the damage Mr Goyle might do could never trouble his conviction of the Higher Good.

His outlook was assured and simple. He knew the truth: what he knew was true. Like David's his idea of rebutting an argument was to include your objections in a restatement of his assertion, 'As you say, two cannot equal four, but all the same two is very variable, and four is twice as variable as two...' Chaudhuri was right, logic is a dead letter outside Europe. Thus our conversation was lengthy and unprogressive, a thoroughly Indian conversation. Because he had done more reading than thinking his head was full, not quite of ideas, but of maxims gleaned from Aurobindo's writings, which served him for bridges over any little difficulties the world of actual experience might present. 'Nature chisels and moulds, so there has to be pain.' 'The seer looks at pain and laughs.' That's the problem of pain dealt with. Our wandering conversation touched too, as is inevitable between a European and an Indian who resents that India's early magnificence is unknown to Europeans, on the culture and omniscience of prehistoric India. But nothing is known of it, I said. Seas of butter. He smiled (he was an exceptionally good-tempered man): television, airplanes, they had invented them all in early days beside the Indus, and had allowed them to lapse because of their triviality compared with the search for wisdom. Why, I asked, had archaeologists never come on traces of these things? Because, he replied, an archaeologist cannot discover the remains of a technology his own era isn't familiar with – how could a nineteenth-century excavator recognise the remains of a television set? – so all India's early wizardry had been shovelled onto the spoil-heap by ignorant Westerners.

When he left me – concerned equally with catering and First Causes he had business in the kitchen – I found that I liked and respected him. I should have expected to feel irritated by his want of rigour, exasperated by his *non sequitur* mind, glad to see the back of him. Instead, with rather the same surprise as I had felt in liking His Highness at Faridkot, I found I rather admired Mr Goyle.

Nonetheless, once alone, I unpacked only what I needed for one night. In the wardrobe the single hanger came from Mary Quant's Ginger Group in the King's Road, which sketched for me the room's previous occupant. What company to keep! I brushed my teeth and spat out toothpaste, surprised to feel it next moment dribbling onto my toes. I looked under the basin: its outlet was not connected to any waste pipe. My toothpaste wound its way across the floor, a caterpillar of bubbles, until it reached a crevice beneath the shower. I washed my feet and went to bed, my mind made up. I would leave in the morning.

In the morning I lay awake in my cell listening to the bustling tick of a kitchen clock which I had noticed nailed up on a prominent beam above the veranda outside my door. Last night Mr Goyle had dismissed my attack on India's want of a coherent history by asserting that the human time-scale of the West was too puny a measure with which to rope and bind the purposes which Divine Wisdom had in mind for India. Tick-tock went the clock, roping time and binding it, then struck eight loud enough to wake the dead. Eight o'clock was the breakfast hour in rue Suffren. I pictured Mr Goyle, caterer as well as counsellor, wringing his hands over the need to reconcile breakfast-time with eternity and, defeated by the conundrum, ascending a ladder to nail up his clock...Or maybe not, maybe it was only the West-trained mind that saw a difficulty put in its path by the contradictions of logic, where no difficulty for Mr Goyle existed. I got up promptly to oblige him as caterer, and after breakfast put off telling him I wasn't staying because he pushed two or three of Aurobindo's books into my hand with a confidence I didn't want to disappoint. I stacked them in my room and went for a walk. Where would I go if I left Pondicherry? I walked through the broad severe streets of the

French town to an esplanade which the sea thumped with dull fury. In either direction, shrouding the measureless strand in mist, hung a smoke of spindrift from the rollers' breaking crests. Yesterday, driving from Madras, my taximan had stopped at Silversands Beach Colony for lunch. It was a straggle of thatched huts sheltered in the dunes of an immense surf-pounded beach. The wind blew not in gusts but with solid unremitting force off the Bay of Bengal. An English family with their Indian ayah were bathing from their establishment of chairs and wind-rocked umbrellas, struggling under towels to take off their clothes decently, emerging at last in the two-piece bathing dresses of the 1950s to skitter through hot sand to the thundering sea. Bathing – the Western idea planted on an Indian shore. Out to sea was the Indian idea: in troughs of the swell, now glimpsed, now gone, sped the sleek windbeaten shapes of little low fishing craft under a lateen sail, taut canvas, glistening black figures, an image at one with wind and sea, man hand in hand with his dangerous companion, like the scribble of a skier racing down alone through a vastness of snow. Yesterday at Silversands the extent and dullness of sea and sand had depressed me, as it did viewed from the esplanade at Pondicherry today. 'The coast of Coromandel, where the early pumpkins blow': Lear's most tragic nonsense. Yesterday I'd been able to tell the taxi to drive on, to leave Silversands behind, but in Pondicherry I had arrived. It was my destination.

If I left, where would I go? Back to the North, back to Jorbagh? If I went back to David and the Delhi life he had showed me I would be agreeing to what his sibylline smile had claimed when I had asserted in face of his idleness that I was a novelist. Then where are the novels, apart from *Try Pleasure*? 'Try pleasure, which, when no other enemy survives, still conquers all the conquerors.' If he was the Indian in the book, repeating Denham's verse, then I was the protagonist who tried to get away from its truth, and failed. I thought of David's two cousins who whiled their lives away playing billiards in Hyderabad. Even as an undergraduate playing billiards all afternoon against David in the Pitt Club, I had thought it a faintly comic pastiche of Edwardian life, like wearing spats, whilst he had taken it seriously – for both of us. It had reminded him of home. So had *thé dansant* at the Dorothy Café for heaven's sake. So had the Cambridge laundry. And the Cambridge Botanical Gardens had reminded him that his grandmother 'boasted an electric rock garden'. I returned through the streets to rue Suffren and re-entered Mr Goyle's domain.

Nothing had changed for the better. My bag was still half-packed, the books Mr Goyle had lent me were still on the table; no decision had been made for me. If I stayed, what would I do? Write? On the table with Aurobindo's books was a note-book I had carried with me every day in India to preserve my jottings and note-takings of anything and everything that had seemed distinctive or significant in the Indian scene: names of trees and birds, pieces of dialogue, phrases used by David and others I had met, anything that struck me as holding in it a drop or two of the essence of place or people. I read a few pages. I had thought of these notes as containing between them the raw material of the novel about India I assumed I would write in response to the intense interest roused in me by my trip so far. But they were scraps, insubstantial, in themselves use-less; as well try and put summer together from a handful of dead flowers. Besides the lists there were snips of scenes, sketches made at the time such as the one I had scribbled down of the English encampment bathing on the Indian shore. But they did not connect. They were illustrations for a book which did not exist. Writing them down in my notebook was not making use of them, not deploying them to serve a purpose. What was missing was an idea, a purpose, a theme to which these scribblings would become concentric, as the scratches in silver are made concentric to the reflection of a light held over its surface.

So the novelist's busy note-taking which had separated me from David's idleness was self-deception. From this I awoke in my Pondicherry oubliette. 'Si quelquefois, sur les marches d'un palais, vous vous réveillez, l'ivresse déjà diminuée ou disparue, demandez à la vague, à l'horloge, demandez quelle heure il est...' I had heard what the waves said, and I could not avoid in this sunless cell the ticking of Mr Goyle's clock. Time passed. Outside in the courtyard sandalled feet came and went. To escape my thoughts I sat at the table, where just enough light for reading glimmered down through the shutters, and drew towards me the top book in the pile of Aurobindo's writings which Mr Goyle had lent me. It was *Adventures in Consciousness*, which I opened. A miasma of sleepiness seemed to rise from the page. I succumbed to it and meditated deeply, my head on my arms as if asleep.

Mr Goyle woke me. He had entered my room at the head of his staff. I have the dreamlike impression that no word was spoken, that I was not consulted, but that he, directing his men with a wave of his hand like the sheriff distraining a bankrupt's chattels, caused everything that was mine in that room to be whisked onto someone's head before leading the troop of bearers into the courtyard, up an outdoor stairway to an upper terrace, then between open shutters into a light and airy room among the rooftops of the town. Here the Indians put down their burdens and stole away, feet pattering down the stone stair which now isolated me from the communal life below. Mr Goyle showed me the view in all directions, and particularly the view onto the heads of unaware passers-by in the street below – he had a way of presenting actuality as if it were his own invention – before putting a book into my hand and vanishing.

It was an impressive performance. Of course he had made me grateful for elevation and freedom by having kept me first in the dungeon below, but, however he did it and for whatever reasons, he kept me from leaving. He led me, if not to Assisi, to a similar sanctuary. As well as a fresh room he tried me with a fresh line in books: the volume he had left me with this time was Edward Carpenter's *Civilisation: Its Cause and Cure*. Everything in Mr Goyle's library, I felt sure, was a thousand pages long and had a momentous title. No use waiting for something handier. I began upon Carpenter with fresh energy.

The solo traveller is at liberty to make what he likes of what he sees, his imagination free, for instance, to finger the view from a train, or to supply the dialogue between two people he sees meeting in the street below his terrace, or to guess at the thoughts of a man polishing his spectacles at a café table. Right or wrong, the world he travels through is a world very largely his own creation. He collects the slides for his own magic lantern show. Quite different is the case of the foreigner in the hands of a native, who will screen the show of his choice, and make his visitor accept its veracity. In Pondy Mr Goyle was the impresario.

Of the cast of characters who lodged with him the first propelled upstairs by Mr Goyle to knock on my door was a Welshman, one half of a stocky couple whom I had already met on the stairs, the wife mannish with short cropped hair and an aggressive line in questioning – Who was I? What did I do? Whom did I know? – while her husband stood by and said nothing, grasping and regrasping the bannister like a retired gymnast contemplating the handsprings of yesteryear. Now, following his knock, he toddled in. Small, in a short-sleeved shirt and trousers belted under his armpits, a few silver hairs laid out on his large head like the fish laid out to dry on the roads round Pondicherry, he climbed onto a chair and examined his glasses before putting them on and turning them in my direction. Then he addressed me. Subject: himself. Duration: an eternity. Abandoned as a terminal case under six separate headings by Welsh doctors in 1931 he had cured himself by his discovery of control via breathing. This triumph, handsomely endorsed by voices and visions, as well as by poems taken down as they were posted into his letter-box head by a divine hand, had encouraged him to set up shop as a faith healer in Borth-y-Gest. He spoke of himself zealously, but without self-righteousness, and it was only by catching at hints that a listener understood his eminence. 'They asked me to take the chair' or 'I said to the President, straight out like, what is the difference between positive-nothing and negative-nothing, eh?' Attempts to move him off the subject of himself were a failure. Ashram politics he had no time for, comparing the jockeying for position in anticipation of the Mother's demise – she was then ninety-five – unfavourably with his own wisdom in having avoided a war of succession by promoting Borth-y-Gest high-flyers into top positions already. For his health, despite breath control, was poor, placing him so often at death's door that he spoke of the doorstep as a familiar perch, and of the House behind the door as if he had the key to it in his pocket, and could go in and out at his pleasure.

What was I to make of him? Undoubtedly Mr Goyle had sent him up, but with what purpose? A grappling-hook flung out to attach me to the fleet? As an enchanter, to draw me under a spell? To bore me to death? Listening to the unending musical voice, I was reminded of the plaintive spiral of supplication I had heard ascending from the Theosophical Society's HQ, which had suggested a soul imprisoned within.

I always feel I am the prisoner of any place until I have found out how to leave it. I need to locate the exit before I can settle in. I walked the French streets and the Indian lanes, but in Pondy I could find no railway station, and no boats appeared from the sea. I saw no signs of arrival or departure, except a travel agent's office. This I visited. Wearing a smile like Mr Goyle's the clerk easily showed me that to leave Pondicherry by any of the means I suggested was next to impossible. His advice, if I wanted to go anywhere, was like the Irish tinker's: don't start from here.

Discouraged, I was driven by the heat to return to rue Suffren and climb upstairs to my terrace. From early morning the heat was terrific, afternoons spent prostrate, the green-shuttered shade of my rooftop room afloat in the dazzle of sunlight like the pad of a lily amidst the dazzle of lake-light. Evening brought life into the streets, which I watched from above. Mr

Goyle had given me a cell with a view. My vantage point was like the gift of insight, the way I could look down unseen into people's lives. There was constant entertainment in the street below. When the milkman made his round with two pails balancing his yoke, those who wanted milk let down jug or bottle on a string from their window and drew up the receptacle full. Lolling schoolgirls with black plaits were delivered to their doors by rickshaw men who had pulled them and their schoolbooks through the town at a trot which made skinny limbs glisten. Young Indian men hurried along the street with transistors pressed to their heads like a remedy for neuralgia; and the tinny noise of radios, mixed with the crackle of static, resounded everywhere from the streets and from open windows. I used to lean on the warm brick of my terrace wall watching for the return from work of a robed official, a judge, a very black stout personage with a bald patch and a briefcase as large as a suitcase which he clasped to himself as he stepped with a show of pomp out of his rickshaw and waddled to his front door. He neither knocked nor rang but waited for it to be opened to him by a servant from within. I fancied a gloom fell on the house with his return, radios shut off, voices sunk to whispers, meals with him a penance for his family. My view from above, my Goyle-given crow's-nest, seemed to provide more than the appearance of things, it seemed to give me perception. I felt possessed of the facility to dissect, first step towards the enabling power a writer has, of re-creation from what he has dissected. Was that the point of the place, why I was here, why Mr Goyle had isolated me among the rooftops?

I didn't give up planning to escape, but, rather against my will, I began to settle in. A routine, reading and excursions, developed of its own accord. Without intending it, by now and again taking a cycle-rickshaw about town I acquired a private chauffeur, a lanky fellow always reclining in his machine when I stepped through the wicket in the street door into rue Suffren, who then sprang out, dusting the seat enticingly with the tail of his dhoti, waving me into it with half-servile, half-menacing gestures, pedalling along close behind me screaming insults if I dared to walk. The rickshaw pullers were a volatile mob, often calling themselves out on strike and running about the streets shaking sticks over their heads. Mr Goyle explained their attitude as the result of the Pope (many of the rickshaw men were Christians) stirring the pot out of jealousy of the authority of Aurobindo and the Mother.

Pope's influence or Mother's, a concealed power was at work in the rumour-ridden town, sinister because it didn't show itself, like some unseen tyrant whose eyes looked in at every window and whose ears listened behind every door. Where was the source of the tyrant's power? There was an Ashram Centre, a community building staffed by mild enough folk, though the notices pinned to its walls were stiffened by a peremptory tone which turned advice into orders and suggestions into commands. There were hints, too, of Utopianism; a model of the Ideal City, Auroville, gleamed under a dome of glass. Was it the centre of the cult's power at Auroville, a few miles from Pondicherry? As I studied the model in the Information Centre an acolyte pushed a pamphlet into my hands offering daily visits to that New Jerusalem. I drew back and escaped in my private rickshaw.

I did not want to be involved. I rode back to rue Suffren and climbed to my vantage-point above the town. At six o'clock the sun sank rapidly, and evening after evening I watched the sky flame briefly behind tow-headed palms whose fronds rattled in the onshore wind blowing a crowd of rooks into black tatters overhead. Darkness fell and I read the books Mr Goyle gave me, or watched the lamplit street below.

At that hour I was a sitting target for Mr Goyle, whose sandals I often heard slapping up the stairs, followed by his benign presence spreading through my quarters like spilled honey. First he would ask me if I lacked anything, any little comfort? Yes, I might reply, an ashtray please. Going to the head of the stair he would call the idea down into the depths below. In a few minutes one of his slender helpers would appear carrying in both hands a bar of soap, or a towel, or a copy of *The Life Divine*. Mr Goyle would break off his talk on Higher Wisdom to scold the servant, sending him back as often as was necessary before an ashtray made its appearance. Never under any pressure of urgency or exasperation did I see Mr Goyle lift a finger himself: he gave orders, and he sat and talked. He told me many things. He told me that his first sight of Aurobindo had been as overwhelming as his first view of the sea. He told me how Aurobindo had given Mr Churchill spiritual aid only for the duration of the 'Hitler war' because, whilst Churchill was a bad man but good for India – he was a proposition in the dialectic of freedom – Hitler was so irredeemably bad that he was anti-evolutionary. So the sage of Pondicherry won the war for Churchill, but in 1945 withdrew his angels so that Churchill lost the General Election and made way for Mr Attlee, who, wishing only for the Raj to vanish, gave India to freedom and to Aurobindo. There was a distance between Mr Goyle and the world, so that his expositions took some time to deliver, his thoughts lost on their travels to hover in the middle air like cherubims wondering why they had begun their descent. By this time the ashtray might at last have been brought, and Mr Goyle, having seen it placed where it was wanted, would paddle off downstairs shooing the servant before him.

His persistent company was kindness for what he saw as the isolation of the outsider. But isolation was what I clung to, dodging all envoys of the central power. I wanted to have no connection shackled on me. When I had been a week at rue Suffren, needing to have some shirts washed I took them to the ashram laundry, as directed by Mr Goyle, and gave them to a clerk who inscribed their dimensions in a ledger. Then he wrote on a ticket the number he had assigned to me, and pushed the ticket at me, saying 'This will be your number always.' Always! I tore up the ticket in the street. Shan't be here long enough to need another shirt washed, I assured myself.

But I was. Day by day I stayed on, walking the blistering streets, pondering all I saw and all I read. At first I walked on the beach too, with the sullen thunder of the surf in my ears, but the beach was made beastly by human excrement, especially by the tide-edge excrement of little colonies I noticed encamped among the sand dunes. When Mr Goyle told me that these were leper colonies I ceased to walk on the sands. But I kept near to the sea, I couldn't keep away, the gleams of light on its vast emptiness attracting me, *ce rire énorme de la mer.*

I was getting nowhere, heat and monotony leaching energy out of me. Defeat. I might as well go back to North India, to the life David had showed me – the idle life he insisted was mine as certainly and as fatally as it was his. If you are a writer, then where, my dear fellow, are the books? That sceptical smile – *ce rire énorme de l'homme vaincu.* And the smile was justified: here I was in Pondy pen in hand, writing nothing, wasting time. I might as well be in Hyderabad playing billiards with David's cousins.

There was a bookshop in the town, which I used to visit on account of the little fellow who kept it. This scrap of zealotry laid frail fingers like empty gloves on your arms and spoke in accents mild, yet generated in his eyes a fire of eagerness for all the world to become just and faithful by way of reading. He knew the right books. He pushed them into my hands, into my pockets, into the basket of the bicycle lent me by Mr Goyle. He would do anything to get a book read; as to whether he sold it or not he was indifferent. In his garden were chairs where passers-by might sit drinking tea free of charge so long as they read. He was saintly, and doomed to the saint's disappointments.

I was a disappointment to him. While the shop in principle stocked only works by or about Aurobindo or the Mother, books would be admitted if they mentioned these two – or so thought the bookshelf elf, licking his pencil with a tiny tongue before writing down the name of a book of Christopher Isherwood's I had mentioned. As he wrote I noticed beneath a pile of sacred literature the heat-curled cover of a paperback. I could read only the second half of each of the two title words: *...am...ede*. Could it be? I reached out as if to consult the top book of the stack, Aurobindo's *Thoughts and Aphorisms*, thus disturbing the pile so that the paperback's full title was revealed to me. *Adam Bede* by George Eliot. Had I been a lonely school-boy and the book a mother's letter, I couldn't have been more anxious to read it. But stealth was needed if the book was not to be picked up with tongs and dropped into a furnace. I turned down tea. I turned down his offer of *Synthesis of Yoga* to read there and then, in a long chair in his garden, saying that I was too tired to do it justice. Picking up three or four of the sage's works I secreted *Adam Bede* among them, jam between doorsteps of bread, and handed him the sandwich to wrap. Though he hesitated at the novel he distressed himself over my choice of books for another reason, that I was taking only Philosophy, whilst what I lacked was Faith. I bicycled away into the heat and left him on tiptoe in the shop doorway, an offered book, as ever, in each hand.

I don't think I ever enjoyed a novel more thoroughly than I enjoyed *Adam Bede* in my upstairs room at rue Suffren. It *was* a work of Faith. I had a kind of hunger which fed on the solidness of the world George Eliot had constructed, after the flimsiness of the ashram writings. The sunset flared behind the palms, the crows cawed at my window, the mosquitoes drank from my veins – but I was ten thousand miles away in Burge's carpenter's shop, and following the men out to hear Dinah preach, and wondering who might be the stranger on horse-back in the circle of her audience on the village green. That evening, eating my supper to solemn music in the dining-room, I thought to myself, how does she do it? Why is that opening more than the mere facts make it? Of course it is accurately observed and well written, but so are lesser books, and the stories in a hundred magazines. This is more. Imagination guided by intellect makes the writer's eye selective, and interlocks the characters, and gives the figures their quiet largeness, and suggests mystery. It was not a result achieved by filling notebooks with observations and hoping a novel would write itself from that material. It was an outcome achieved by design, and by balance, and by all the writer's gifts marshalled and led by the intentions of a clear intellect.

I returned to the components of a novel, drafted before I left England, and now reconsidered. This hard work banished the sense of wasting time, most pernicious of sorrows, and distanced me from the incursions and agitations of rue Suffren. In leisure intervals I walked about the town, and continued my researches into how to reach Cochin, and, when at home, enjoyed the vagaries of Mr Goyle and his residents. They didn't impinge on the work at the writing table, which conferred its blissful serenity.

One evening when I came home and climbed the stairs I found lounging in a wicker chair on my terrace a young American ashramite I had known since my arrival, the cousin of a friend, who had called on me in my first days and now dropped in from time to time to talk. He was tall and laid-back, in loose Indian clothes, and he merely raised a hand in silent greeting. I liked him, welcomed his visits. On the surface he was a soft-spoken, easy-going Ivy Leaguer in his late twenties, as anxious to listen as to talk, picking his words with care. Because he wore tinted glasses his eyes weren't on show, which gave the impression of reserve. He had told me how he had crossed India by train from Bombay on first arrival, abandoning his air-conditioned first-class sleeper (booked from America) in favour of travelling outside among Indian clingers-on, to get him a feel of the *real* India. That had been years ago: he had come and gone many times since. His cool likeability made me more interested in the ashram and in Aurobindo than did the effusions of emotional disciples: he gave the impression of not trying to cut any ice, of knowing something he didn't need to tell. He would talk of the ashram, and of the society which had formed round it, with a kind of detached candour which seemed indifferent to suffering caused by the society's rules or habits; his philanthropy was for mankind rather than for the individual. When I told him about the miseries of the rue Suffren cook, Michou, he replied yes, marriages most often broke up in the ashram and affairs were common, the usual pattern only a few days from take-off to bust-up. Nearly everyone in the place had hepatitis. Death was common, drugs rife. He sounded like an anthropologist picking up specimens with tweezers. Yet he had stayed American enough at heart to believe that dollars spent improving the drains in Tamil villages were dollars spent redeeming mankind. He was tolerant of me too, though I doubt if he liked me.

When I came up the stairway that hot evening, and found him watching the rooks from a terrace chair, I had been on my ramble wrestling with the conundrum of where to go, and how to get there, when I left Pondicherry. I walked about expounding to him the difficulties in my way. I can't get to Cochin, I said. No plane, no train, a taxi would cost a fortune. If not Cochin, where? The travel agent's advice is to backtrack to Madras. Don't start from here, he says.

'There is a way.' He spoke quietly out of the dark.

'Oh, what way's that?'

'You just walk out the door. India'll take care of you.'

I thought about his advice after he'd gone. It was not a travel policy I could formulate for myself, especially vis-à-vis India. Italy perhaps I could trust in that way, but not Asia, not unknown India. Besides, I had too much baggage.

Mr Goyle in his kindness continued offering me whatever he believed would show me the path. One day it was the *Gita*, another it was bread. He concerned himself about the little I ate, calling me into his larder to make free with anything on its shelves. Once he took down a tin labelled POWER which he fingered thoughtfully before replacing it, as if he had forgotten its purpose. Another evening he brought up to my terrace a woman of a certain age whom I had noticed eating alone with an air of self-sufficiency in a choice corner of the dining room. He introduced her as 'Marta' only – surnames were discarded as excess baggage in rue Suffren – but he thought the case exceptional enough to add 'She is contessa, you know, a great lady,' In the doorway Marta waved a hand, 'Oh, title is nothing.'

But the style that went with it wasn't nothing. In she came, a rustling, assured person *di buona famiglia*, and took a chair at the window where the evening light could halo well-kept hair. The surprise of stylishness in rue Suffren, her worldly stylishness evident in that easy manner, that rich tone, the gracefully managed silks of her clothes – it was a lovely surprise. We shared friends in Rome, and I heard their names with a feeling of homesickness...one name above others, of a woman who had been a rue Suffren inmate until a month ago, when she had been sacked. Sacked? Marta laughed. Whatever entreaties Mr Goyle had made, whatever Aurobindo-based arguments for modesty he had put forward, this woman had continued painting the courtyard balcony wearing a bikini up the ladder, like a ceiling-angel in a baroque fresco. The Welsh wife complained. Mr Goyle wrung his hands. She left, and the sky above rue Suffren darkened, to lighten above her wherever she went. High spirits and optimism had carried her through many storms, piratical colours flying. I heard Marta extolling her dedication to the Buddha, her retreat into the sanctity of the Himalayas. I sat listening in my courtly manner, and thought of her in Rome, or in a box at Epsom, or playing rummy in Oughterard ... always herself, always the enthusiast, always with the reckless streak which mocks authority. Of course she had plunged heart and mind into a passion for Aurobindo. Postcards used to come in from her, posted in every corner of the world, each freighted with a passion for some new thing. 'Hi, Philip, I'm on Cloud Nine...' I had a feeling that she and I had seen too much of each other elsewhere to be able to believe in each other here.

The idea of her in rue Suffren, a ceiling-angel on Cloud Nine with her paint-pot, let a seep of restlessness into my mind. It prevented work. Once noticed, the electric pump which filled water tanks on my terrace began to drill into my mind. The crows peering in through my window made me uneasy. Irritations swarmed like the mosquitoes. Mr Goyle, asked for the cricket score (an English side was touring India), replied 'Yesterday England was having its chance, today India is trying, so tomorrow we shall see.' It was the same wool that filled Aurobindo's books. It was the sort of stuff the travel agent fed me. It was why life in Pondicherry was like the struggles of an ant in treacle. Then, out of these irritations, the fatal question formed itself: *Que diable allais-je faire dans cette galère?*

Before I left Pondicherry I was curious to see the city of Auroville. I had gazed at its model under glass in the Ashram Centre. I had heard its name pronounced with the certainty and reverence of a believer speaking of the New Jerusalem. With expectations as free of scepticism as was possible I booked myself in for a tour.

The group assembled outside the Ashram Centre and boarded a bus in the charge of a young Frenchman. A red dust road led away from Pondicherry, at first through groves of cashew and lemon, then between plantations of the small but delectable bananas which Mr Goyle supplied me with, until we reached a wide sandy plateau of wind and sun and distance scattered with Tamil villages, the Bay of Bengal a cobalt line beyond. In this ancient and beautiful landscape the first sign of the coming city was a concrete byre for fifty hand-milked cows, and the first hint of what we could expect from our guide was that he told us the name of the byre's architect, spelling it so that it would not be handed down by us in a corrupt reading when we came to tell our children's children how we had visited The City.

When our bus stopped at the site of Auroville-to-be we alighted as if from a spacecraft into a prospect which might have been the preparations for building a city on another planet. Men and women moved through a pitted and scarred landscape with a sleep-walker's solemnity, wheeling barrows, ascending earth stairways with sacks on their heads, chipping high-mindedly at the ground with mattocks. Westerners and Indians worked side by side. They were building with their hands the city they believed in, which existed already in their heads. Our bus had whizzed through the galaxy and landed us amongst the believers.

Warning us to take off our shoes, our guide led us first into the House of Aurosun, a hut in which Auroville's first child was born, an event half legendary, half real, which struck a dreamy note the whole place sustained. Auroville! It resembled all the other outpourings of Aurobindo's mind: even though I could see it and walk in it I couldn't quite believe in it, the same way you can accept a metaphysical proposition but baulk at trusting your physical weight to it. In fact all I saw, this half-baked actuality, made criticism of Aurobindo's metaphysics more cogent. I had thought that by antipathy for Aurobindo I might be missing something; when I saw Auroville I saw what I had missed. Through dust and devastation our guide floated at his priestly pace and we followed, a huddle of earthlings anxious not to trip. We were shown huts with shining floors where long-haired young men and women sat cross-legged and regarded us incuriously through stoned eyes. We were shown scratches in the dust towards which the guide waved his magician's arm: 'Ici le théâtre. It is air-conditioned, also the restaurant can be there. And here is all gardens,' – a half acre of sand – 'we have the flowers ready.' He could not tell the difference between what is, what was, or what might be: it was not in this ordered way that he spoke of time. That no distinction was allowed between past, present and future was what gave the site and the project its surrealism. Flowers came before gardens, everywhere the end before the means, the applause before the achievement. It was like children building on the nursery carpet. At the meteorological station the guide told us, 'Here we make the weather change.' Cause and effect were reversed too.

Yet in it all there was a touch of ice; not such happy children, in the power of a Mother whose wishes altered the climate. I could imagine the slaves who built Mitla, or dragged the monoliths to Stonehenge, working with the same dead-eyed dedication for a fanatical power which had stolen their minds by emptying them of everything except herself. It was, or would be, the Mother's city. At the heart of the site we looked into the pit from which would rise the city's chief building, the Matrimandir. In this pit – hollowed by mattocks and fingernails so that no bulldozer ravished mother earth – would be founded the matrix. 'Rising from the earth-crater like a hidden sun [I quote from *Auroville Perspective*] the Matrimandir unfolds the living soul of Auroville. A column of light pours through an aperture above, penetrating its inmost heart to the depths below: two movements of consciousness, one ascending, opening from within, the other descending, quickening the seed. The Matrimandir is both the symbol and embodiment of Auroville's aspiration for the Truth, that luminous point from which the city rays forth.'

Actually, the Matrimandir was presently a hole chipped in the ground. The site, with its trenches and furrows, resembled at that time an archaeological excavation in search of a lost city of the past quite as much as the foundation work for a city of the future. From these scratchings our guide talked up theatres and conference halls just as the cruise-ship guide might talk up the topless towers of Ilium out of a mound on a Turkish plain. In a sense the site of Auroville was an excavation: an excavation of mankind's path in order to unearth the crossroad at which he had taken the wrong turning – had mistaken, according to Aurobindo, inaction for nirvana – and from that point to begin building again.

In the bus back to Planet Earth I resolved to leave Pondy at once. Auroville made clear much that was usually wrapped in impenetrable verbiage. Where the purpose of the weather station was said in Aurospeak 'to implement a metamorphosis in the metabolism of the biosphere', our guide put it more succinctly: the weather station's job was to change the weather. There was an innocence about the woolly language which the succinct version lost, and replaced with the staccato orders of a tyrant of unreason. Her traps were set. Even Mr Goyle stalked her victims for her, sidling about rue Suffren as quietly as a spider. One moment the visitor would be sitting in Mr Goyle's pantry, discussing *Rodogune* (an Aurobindo tragedy in five acts), the next he would find himself in shorts with waist-length hair, chipping away in that infernal pit with a mattock his only possession. I determined to get out before the spider struck, telling no one my plans.

But Mr Goyle knew what I had in mind, just as though he had read it in the paper. The travel agent was to book me a car and driver to take me back to the Connemara at Madras, from which point I could begin again, and re-enter the real world as though Pondicherry had been a dream. Mr Goyle called me into his pantry. He had managed to prise the lid off the tin labelled POWER and he offered me a drink made from its contents. 'It will give you the strength to cycle to the bus station.'

'Bus station? I didn't know there was one.'

'It is how you will go.'

'Does a bus go to Cochin?'

'The bus will take you where you go.'

He took a biscuit from a drawer and gave it to me. We talked in the way we had fallen into the habit of talking, he dealing in dreams with cryptic portentousness, myself yapping at his heels. Because I thought I should speak my mind before I left, I warned him (thinking of my friend whose wife and children had fallen into the community's clutches) that those who have elected to follow the 'householder's' path (or who find themselves householders more or less by default, like so many who never planned life out) do not have chiefly their own salvation to consider; they have created by their own action an entity (a union, a marriage, a family) for which they are responsible – an entity which is more important than any one of its constituents severally. I said I quite believed that the miseries of this world, poverty, neglect, loneliness, may be regarded with calm, even with joy at the opportunities offered to display virtue, by the yogin who sees Brahmin in everything; but so to regard the misery of another, when you have been its cause, I would never believe to be virtuous. Having chosen the householder's way, even mistakenly, you must not defect but shoulder its burdens as best you can. He claimed that the yogin, married or single, spreads joy around him. I told him he ignored the facts of married life as well as the statistics of divorce: yogins' marriages, like Aurobindo's own, are usually miserable enough to end in divorce. When Mr Goyle fell silent I wondered if *he* had been married and divorced. Familiar as I was with his mind, I knew nothing of his history, except that he had once owned a factory in Calcutta ...less long a stride is required of an Indian who gives up his factory for an ashram than the stride required of a Westerner to carry him across such a chasm. No doubt he had meditated in the factory just as he added up money at the ashram. I asked him how he had known that I was leaving. He answered, as usual, with an effect rather than a cause: 'I told a lady inquiring for a room that I will have a vacancy on Thursday.' I finished the POWER and borrowed his bike to make inquiry at the bus station.

Nine

I woke myself in rue Suffren before even the crows were astir, and crept downstairs with my baggage at 4.30 am. Michou the cook opened the wicket-door for me, and I stepped out into the street. My rickshaw walla, sprawled in his vehicle, was soon awake and pedalling me through a sleeping town. Mr Goyle had stretched out his hand in farewell by sending ahead a rue Suffren servant to greet me at the bus station and guide my rickshaw among the slumbering monsters to the place where the bus to Bangalore was being wakened and readied for its run. Behind a radiator already garlanded with marigolds, men were splashing the auspicious *kunkum* on its windscreen and headlamps. Glassless except for this cracked windscreen, its body bulging with people under a roof stacked with luggage, the bus groaned like a loaded camel being forced to its feet as the driver turned over the engine. I paid off my rickshaw and climbed aboard whilst agile boys secured my luggage to the roof. Through the window the rue Suffren servant handed me up a cotton bag woven with a fortunate design, a last kindness from Mr Goyle in which he had placed biscuits, bananas and a copy of *The Life Divine*.

At 5.30 away we rattled with a fierce roar into the dark, the wind of speed chilly at the windows, through streets full of wrapped shapes asleep on pavement or *pyol*. Finally, smashing our way through a busy lantern-lit bazaar, we gained the open country, and, settling down to a jog-trot across the plains, found ourselves in the midst of the vast lavatory that rural India becomes with each dawn, men squatting in every field and tank and riverbed, women (earlier risers) entirely absent from the scene.

There were about seventy people aboard the bus, crushed together like the crowd in a rush-hour tube. It was a social mix. No doubt the poorest class wasn't present, though a more or less naked beggar sat next me for one stage and nudged me and poked me with that whispering persistence which will harden the most charitable heart. At another time there was an ugly bourgeois gent in a brown suit on board, evidently proud of his English, who put me through an interrogation shouted from the other end of the bus. Everyone listened, watching me with placid brown eyes which were without either animosity or sympathy. The beggar saw me as a mark, the babu saw me as a means of showing off, the youth beside me saw me as a headrest; but none of them showed a scrap of interest in the foreigner amongst them.

This Indian indifference makes travelling in India comfortably anonymous. Now and then I was stared at, of course, by small naked children walking backwards ahead of me whenever I got off the bus to stretch my legs in a village street, but on the whole I was ignored, as the traveller longs to be, so that he may watch and listen and be comfortable in himself. Once you are noticed, you come into uncomfortable existence, like a discovered earwig. When David and I had stopped in a village on the way back from Jaipur we had been as much of an event as a travelling sideshow, and the intentness with which we had been watched was a force isolating us. Through the tinted glass and air-conditioning of the tourist's isolation the brilliance and heat of India, like its poverty and dirt, look alien and threatening. I had expected it to look like that to me, once I left rue Suffren. But all that long day, thirteen hours in the Bangalore-bound bus, I loved the way India looked. As well as the food which his emissary had put into my hands for the journey, Mr Goyle had put sustenance into my head.

To enjoy a bus ride across South India in the heat of the day you need a quiet mind. The journey was hardly thrilling. At the end of every long straight road our bus stopped in every village. Loaded with baggage animate and inanimate it waited. Crows settled on the roof to peck rice from the sacks. A dusty road led in and another led out; a cluster of mud and thatch; cows, goats, dogs, children, a line of the elderly with their gnarled sticks watching from a stone bench in the shade of a peepul tree; a dirty pool, passengers peeing against a mud wall, perhaps an enigmatic statue with a Sanscrit inscription and uplifted eyes; all around, near and far, the glitter of the plains in the heat. In the villages nothing happened. I needed my quiet mind and my few bananas to make me content with the inertia of an Indian village. We waited, but nothing happened. In the towns it was different: in a town bus station our bus was the centre of a vortex of human energy, the target for desperate vendors, to whom bus passengers showed the indifference which the villages had shown to them. We sat ignoring the clamour. It was a buyer's market. Below my window a boy selling ices blasted away shrill and urgent on his klaxon, but no one stirred. Then the driver sprang aboard after refreshing himself with friends, and with a responding roar the bus engine came to life. It was suddenly a seller's market. Immediately, like the waving antennae of a weird creature, a thicket of hands waving grubby money reached out of the windows for ices. It was now the vendor's chance to look lordly and choose his customer, whilst the bus driver, powerful in his turn, paid not the slightest heed to his passengers' unreadiness for departure but pulled away in a pandemonium of screams and fluttering money.

After a day on an unsprung seat the city of Bangalore was welcome. Passengers dissolved into the crowd and the bus was an empty shell, its roof stripped of sacks and bundles. My suitcase, a large Revelation which looked incongruous on the bus roof – and, had it burst, would have showered Bangalore with incongruous items of an Englishman's wardrobe – was pulled down by a team of three teenagers. The eldest ordered his second in command to put it on the third boy's head and we set off Indian file to hunt a taxi like a shikar party trotting into the jungle. A taxi found, they put my luggage into it whilst I asked the price of a ride to the West-End Hotel on Racecourse Road. Self-respect vis-à-vis a foreigner obliged the driver to ask a ridiculous sum, which my own self-respect (I knew from David's company what such things cost an Indian) obliged me to turn down. Impasse. I had my team remove my suitcase from the taxi and find me a rickshaw. This settled, their leader asked for 'porterage, three rupees'. Self: 'Three rupees? For one case? Don't be ridiculous.' Chief porter (waggling his head earnestly): 'Oh but yes, master, for loading, unloading, plus handling charge, three rupees.' Self (getting into rickshaw): 'Here's one rupee. Drive on.' Leaving the three boys to examine my rupee the three-wheeled Lambretta motored away, its driver (on my side for the moment) shouting over his shoulder 'Right price, master.' The day's journey, and it had been a significant journey for me, had cost me in all £1.

I'm not sure that I recognised at once the significance of the journey, or the development wrought in me by my sojourn in rue Suffren. I had arrived in Pondicherry dependent on David's version of Indian reality – plane and taxi – which had carried me to the very doors of the rue Suffren lodging-house. There Mr Goyle's view of the matter took over. I tried to leave by taxi or by air, and failed, and was immobilised until Mr Goyle judged it time to push me off in a bus without attending overmuch to where the bus might take me. I had thought I wanted to go to Cochin, but here I was in Bangalore, as interesting a town as curiosity and patience could make it, or as irksome and dirty and dull a backwater in which an incurious or impatient tourist could find himself stuck. The verdict was up to me.

My mind was not so quietened by Mr Goyle that I didn't look for a way out of Bangalore the moment I found my way in. In the lobby of the hotel was a travel desk, and on Mahatma Gandhi Road Thomas Cook had an office, both of which seemed to offer the machinery for supplying pre-booked train seats and reserved hotel rooms and all the other paraphernalia of planned travel. Take this direction, though, and you fetch up face to face with India's shortcomings. The idea was there, and the machinery, but they weren't plugged in to reality. At the hotel travel desk the chief passed my questions about Goa-bound trains to a clerk who had no idea at all how to read a timetable, and my questions about Goan hotels he passed to another clerk who replied without hesitation that there were no hotel rooms to be had in Goa for as far into the future as anyone could see. I suppose if he had exerted himself the chief could have looked up a train and rung up a hotel, but he was too important to work. He could only delegate. It is, or was, a general Indian characteristic which the head-of-office clerk shared not only with David and with Mr Goyle but with the head boy of the porter team at the bus station too: the moment an Indian is promoted, or promotes himself, he appoints him-self Ruler and refuses the indignity of work, delegating to underlings the tasks which, if he tried his hardest, he might conceivably be capable enough to accomplish himself. It is a matter of self-esteem. No condescension suggested by Debrett can rival the condescension of the Indian babu towards his peon. Of course an Indian customer has peons of his own to send out against the babu's underlings, and to wait in the babu's line, and suffer the babu's peon's ignorance – pawn fighting against pawn while the major pieces slumber unmoved on the back squares.

For it is in order to reach a state of perfect idleness, to slum-ber on a back seat he calls a throne, that the Indian is ambi-tious. Not that he has a use for time thus gained, or a purpose behind his ambition: idleness is beautifully complete, asking nothing more than itself *ad infinitum*. David's life in Delhi, even dhobi-day, was perfectly idle; he had none of the resorts with which a European fills his diary so that his life looks busy to himself and to others. He wanted to see through my pretence of work, my claim to be a writer, in order to see the pure true me existing in the same vacuity as himself. I remembered how he had spoken, almost wistfully, of those cousins of his in

Hyderabad every day and all day playing billiards, as though they were one step nearer Heaven than ourselves.

David's cousins came into my mind because of a group using my hotel in Bangalore as their headquarters. The West-End was rather a comfortable place, Swiss Cottage in style, my room furnished with mahogany, my door giving onto a shaded veranda with a lawn beyond. Here I passed my time reading or writing when I wasn't quizzing the travel agencies or searching the shops for old ivories, and here, to the shade of this verandaed terrace, came Bangalore's fast set. I watched them from my end of the terrace, and I watched them in the dining-room. In particular one young man in his twenties interested me, slight, long-haired, who lounged in his chair tossing from hand to hand the keys of a Mark VII Jaguar I had seen him leave in the car park. Beside him an upright bespectacled Indian youth received the young man's orders – for drinks, for cigarettes, for the maître d'hôtel – and passed the orders to a bearer. Once or twice a girl joined them, dark glasses and headscarf echoing the same sixties style they all aimed for, and they would go indoors to eat. Neither outside nor inside – not over drinks, not over lunch – did they converse. There was no companionship, no conversation, no laughter, just their orders passed via toady to the bearers, and silence. I thought of the silent meals at Faridkot, where the hierarchy made it impossible for anyone but HH or David to initiate conversation. My own discomfort with silence felt like an inadequacy there: to be content with silence, and fulfilled by idleness, would have fitted me better than any conversational powers might have done for an Indian dinner table. But – perhaps because holding your tongue suggests subservience and deference in place of the democracy of lively talk – it goes entirely against the European grain to be content in company with silence. At Cambridge, even in the upper divisions at school, assessment of anybody's cleverness was made by judging the nimbleness of his tongue, and whether or not he was funny, rather than by what he could achieve with his pen in the silence of the examination halls.

Total immersion in the foreign scene, which only happens if you travel alone, submerges the viewpoint. You think yourself radically altered by foreign conditions, permanently changed by influences which retrospect sees as ephemeral. In rue Suffren I had assumed that air seeded with Aurobindo's ruminations was the atmosphere I would continue to breathe after quitting Pondy, just as I couldn't imagine clean clothes coming back from the wash which didn't smell enticingly of India. I thought it would always be like this. I thought I could take India home with me.

One evening I took a tonga through the haphazard sprawl of low-built Bangalore – past the cricket ground, past cows asleep in the roadway – to the Lal Bagh, a park of 240 acres planted with magnificent trees. After walking for an hour or two amongst these Indian giants I sat down on a bench and recorded on the endpaper of my book – it was *One Hundred Beautiful Trees of India* – a list of my favourites, noting the form and habit of each tree beside its name. Nothing odd in that. I believed then that by naming things you in some sense acquire them, or gain control over them, as Adam gained dominion over all creatures by knowing their names, of which Satan had been kept by God in ignorance. But the list of these Indian trees' names is headed 'Trees for Strode'. I thought they would grow in England, around the house we had not yet moved into, forming Indian presences in our landscape. I thought I could take India home with me, that in Dorset I would sit in the shade of a Mysore fig reading Aurobindo's *Hymns to the Mystic Fire*. Now, twenty-eight years later, all that remains of my belief is a stunted podocarpus, victim of snowfall and gale, which just survives in a sheltered wood. It isn't whole trees you bring back with you from other climes: seed, not trees, is what comes home unregistered in the turn-ups of the traveller's trousers to hybridise with native flora.

In the Lal Bagh I had come upon rather a charming equestrian statue, a swaggering affair of prancing hooves and magisterial rider, which was titled simply 'His Highness the Late Maharaja of Mysore' without the dates needed to place his individual lateness within linear history. Of the various destinations open to me, en route for Goa, I decided on the evidence of the statue that Mysore was likely to suit me best. All difficulties of travel melted away: Mysore was where I had always been expected to want to go, the easiest place to go from Bangalore, and the travel desk clerks at the West-End sold me with relief on all three faces a ticket for a first-class chair car to carry me out of their lives. It was a journey of a few hours, seventy or eighty miles. The steam engine with its sonorous bellow drew the long train through a desolate hot land. Here and there the eye was drawn to a coconut grove, or a patch of paddy, or a wood of eucalyptus, but mostly it was a landscape of scrub and cactus and sand, the slopes dotted with the crumbling towers of anthills, all of it shimmering in the eye-tearing Indian light. I was getting used to the Indian landscape and the Indian light. You absorb through your eyes more than you are aware of learning. Once, returning from a long trip in Asia, I found that the foreign scene had imprinted itself so deeply on my mind's eye that the square grey church towers of Kent, and the lanes and fidgety fields seen from the Folkestone train, made England unfamiliar to me. If you absorb the foreign scene by means of what you see through the bus window, you learn a background against which foreign actions and alien characteristics are less of a surprise. When I lived in Italy I learned more about my friends' Italian nature from watching their compatriots' behaviour in the streets than I ever learned direct from themselves. Every day in India I came upon the explanation of something that had puzzled me about David. Once I had asked him some question about his mali's wages, to which he answered (like his granny) elliptically: 'In India it is implements which are costly, labour is nothing.' I pondered this for a moment – the mali didn't seem over-mechanised – and forgot it until, in Bangalore, I came upon a man painting iron railings with his hand. He had no brush. Into the pot he dipped his hand, which emerged glistening to caress the ironwork. What David had meant was that hands are cheaper than brushes. It was an axiom acceptable within the Indian scene: give a man a brush and he'll sell it, and go on painting with his hand. No use feeling indignant. The more you comprehend, the more you pardon.

Still there are surprises. I watched, while the Mysore train waited in a station, an Indian family picnicking on the platform with that serendipity I have often envied: rug spread, mother squatting over the cooking-stove, papa sprawled at ease to play with baby, eight-year-old daughter trotting to the platform edge to empty tea-leaves onto the rails as if the track was a river bearing debris away; the family unit as unconscious of the station crowd as if they were picnicking under the wayside banyan. I watched them packing up their picnic and boarding my coach. The train drew out. Very soon the little girl hurried down the corridor, entered the first-class lavatory and without closing the door squatted down and pee'd on the floor.

The Metropole at Mysore began, as do all hotels with a will of their own, by trying to stop me getting in, and, once in, by adopting the broom cupboard treatment to get me out. 'No, sir, no single rooms vacant.' I said I'd take a double. Lips purse, pencil runs up and down column: 'Well, let's try No.10.' Upstairs the party bundles, clerks giving orders, porters passing them on to bellboys barely able to lift my suitcase. No. 10 is hot, noisy, tiny and dirty – the broom cupboard. I remember David's technique at the Khetri House in Jaipur. 'This won't do at all, show me better rooms.' Desk clerk sends under-clerk downstairs for keys. Now large rooms one after another are opened, grudgingly at first, then with increasing pride as single rooms and doubles and bridal suites of tawdry grandeur are displayed, all empty, all dirty, all hot, all overlaid with a flimsy patina of 'luxury' from a last refurbishment in the satin-draped days of princely Mysore. By the time I chose a room – a single with fourposter on the quiet and shady side of the building – the entire staff, waiters and even cooks as well as clerks, had joined the tour, running from downstairs to press together at the room's door to examine me before trooping off chattering. Alone at last in rather an elegant room, I wondered why they did it – why try and put me in the broom cupboard when hardly another room in the hotel was taken? An entrance test to discover how far my Indian education had proceeded?

If getting in was an entrance test, I was made welcome once I'd passed. It was luxury in the Indian style: basic discomfort ameliorated by sybaritic trimmings. Bed-tea began the day, a tray brought to my bedside and my curtains opened, at any hour that suited the staff no matter what time I had asked to be called. 'Seven o'clock,' announced the imperturbable bearer as he withdrew. He was rarely right. Whatever the real time (probably there was no accurate clock in the place) it suited him to call it seven o'clock. I sometimes ate my dinner in the dining-room, uncovered dishes brought at a smart tramp from distant kitchens, so that the boiled joint, and the potatoes, and the rice pudding would be cold and sticky by the time the bearers had passed it among themselves for the maître himself to place it before me. 'Good appetite,' he always said, making the wish sound like an order. Though solemn, the Metropole was a friendly place. I drank the Mysore beer, and read *Adam Bede* with my meals, and was content.

Mysore was then a little town into which an Englishman could comfortably settle. 'Every inch a princely city' the guide book called it, and, although some inches were more princely than others, its charm was in the Toytown effect given to its streets and squares by statues and fountains and public building poured forth with the extravagance of a princely hand. In Mysore I understood what HH and his predecessors had been aiming for in Faridkot: good works and glory. The Ruler's decoration of his capital was in intention somewhere between a nineteenth-century English squire building a school for his village and a French emperor erecting the Arc de Triomphe. Content to dawdle about the town, I spent even more time resting at a tin table in the shade of the hotel garden, which was divided from the street only by a hedge like an upturned scrubbing-brush, where I read Aurobindo. I still stuck to the discipline of studying the sage's works, relevant to actuality in some degree whilst I could look up from reading at my tin table and watch the Indian world go by. The Metropole garden was always active in some particularly Indian and interesting way: business meetings, assignations, youthful parties, once a wedding reception with music booming from loudspeakers far into the night and a mess in the gardens next morning like the wreckage after a riot. It seemed to me that I was immersed in India, and I was happy. Whence came this peace of mind I didn't inquire. It was loneliness, but loneliness transfigured. No one in the world, save these citizens of Mysore, knew where I was.

I used my tin table in the front garden as a base for my operations, the spot where people I was negotiating with could be sure of finding me. A clerk from the booking office came on foot from the railway station – I was still trying to get to Goa – and stood listening to my ambitions with furrowed brow; but as soon as I finished speaking he would shift his weight from one foot to the other and ask, 'Now, sir, please tell me, where are you hoping to be travelling to?' I think he hoped that if his patience outlasted mine, I would give up Goa and reply 'Bangalore', when he would have whipped out a ticket which took me off his hands. Alternatively, from the wistful way he told me one day that an airport was to be built any year now at Mysore (there was already an 'Aerodrome Office' in the town, proposing the idea of air travel the same way the Auroville weather station proposed an improved climate), he perhaps nursed a hope that I would give up pestering him about trains and live a life of pleasure at the Metropole until air travel came to Mysore – or returned to it, for of course, as I had learned from Mr Goyle, and was reminded daily by Aurobindo, India had invented and discarded the aeroplane many millennia ago.

Another visitor to the Metropole garden was the shopkeeper from the Arts and Crafts Emporium on Sayyaji Rao Road, who arrived by bicycle most days to continue negotiations broken off yesterday over the price of two sets of ivory chessmen I was trying to buy from him. Shopkeepers such as this vendor of ivory bribed every bus tour driver to stop outside their premises. The tourists, mostly local country people, would flock into the shop just as if it were the museum or factory or palace they had paid to visit, and it was by means of a bus tour that I had first visited the Arts and Crafts Emporium myself and shown cautious interest, if the price could be made right, in buying ivory chessmen.

Touts from rival bus firms visited the Metropole garden very frequently. One evening I bought a ticket from the Empire Travels rep for a 'luxury coach' taking in all the sights, and walked to the rendezvous ('oposite Woodland Talkies') at the advertised time, 7.30 next morning. No bus. No one, it seemed, had ever seen a ticket like mine before, and could only wag heads over my misfortune. I waited half an hour, and was walking away reflecting how easily I had been stung, when the ancient vehicle from Empire Travels appeared in a symphony of smoke and rattling metal. I climbed aboard, and soon found I had joined a school treat: thirty-eight ten-year-old schoolboys in the charge of a prefect with a lacy shirt and a cane, behind whom lurked a small fierce schoolmaster with a Hitler moustache. Besides myself there was one tourist only, a very dark barefooted man in a dhoti with the usual woollen scarf wrapped round his neck which denotes a winter wardrobe. Away we rattled to the shops, the driver wrestling a huge wheel, beside him his underling, a half-witted creature, whose duty was to sound the horn.

After three or four stops at shops marketing Mysore's produce (silk and sandalwood as well as ivory) we reached the zoo, where the children stampeded off the bus already screaming with excitement at the ways they proposed to ill-treat the animals. I followed them. But I wasn't so inured to misery as I thought India had made me. I couldn't meet the creatures' eyes for shame and grief. I could ignore the human wreckage begging at the gate easier than I could face the animals. You can always turn a corner in India and come on something in yourself you aren't ready for. I had been making myself too comfortable in Mysore.

The bus needed a push-start but there were plenty of volunteers, an eager group picked out by the ferrule of the prefect's cane. When the engine fired we bumped off out of town into a green and watered land.

The object of the school tour was historical: to visit the sites associated with Tipu Sultan, whose infamous tyranny is forgotten in India – or, if remembered, is forgiven – by virtue of his campaigns against the British. It is almost the only credential that counts in assessing a historical figure: was he or was he not against the British? Can he be claimed as a 'freedom fighter'? Thus a secondary motive is magnified, and a historical picture distorted – in Indian teaching – whilst the history I had been taught erred all the other way, classifying Tipu as a 'rebel' and counting his defeat by Wellesley at Seringapatam as a triumph for the forces of prosperity, order and reform. No bus can have approached Tipu's tomb by the Cauvery river containing views more opposite than were the small fierce schoolmaster's to mine.

The site of Tipu's capital is an island formed between two arms of the Cauvery, here a swift broad river running over rocks and washing the steps of a bathing ghat where we stopped for the children to swim. I sat watching, unnoticed, on the warm stone steps between temple and water. To recognise how much we differed, how little we shared, was a corrective to the comfortable sense of belonging which made the garden of the Metropole so pleasant to me. The trace of Britain's imprint on India, as well as its stigma upon an Indian like David, deceives an Englishman into feeling at home, with friends he understands. Most obviously it is the language – the fact that these boys and their crusty dominie, as well as the barefoot tourist, all spoke some English – but more insidiously a thousand customs and habits, all combine to whisper what is comfortable and familiar in an Englishman's ear. It is false. Better notice what is different. I sat on the ghat steps and remembered all I could about Tipu's career as I had been taught it, and then reinterpreted these 'facts' as I imagined the school-master on another step of the ghat teaching them as 'facts' to his class. Tipu the freedom fighter who still terrifies the English by means of his mechanical tiger devouring a Company sepoy in the V & A...Tipu outwitting Cornwallis, tricking the French, mastering the South, only trapped and killed here in his besieged capital by the weight of arms brought against him. It is Boadicea against the Romans, Harold against the French: partisan history which stirs patriotic blood. In Samarkand, at a moment when a national figurehead was needed for inspiration against Soviet rule, I even heard Tamerlane represented as a leader only concerned to free his people from a foreign yoke.

The Republic Day parade in Delhi had made me wonder if the Oriental mind is constructed to 'believe' history in the same sense that, say, a research-trained German mind believes it. The German, or Western, method may be compared to excavation – a chipped and defaced stone figure of Tipu carefully unearthed, meticulously studied, nothing added, no lost nose replaced or missing limbs supplied – whilst the Oriental, like the European historian prior to the nineteenth century, approaches the past as a sculptor looks to a marble quarry, for the raw material on which to practise his art. He does not in his heart make an absolute separation between myth and history. The historical Tipu, unearthed by the West and placed behind museum glass in a fragmentary condition, is merely the starting-point for the lively figure required by India's reconstruction of her past into a form acceptable to her present. With a little more work, Tipu will qualify for a float of his own in the Republic Day parade through Delhi.

Whatever their teacher told them about Tipu, those school-boys cheered him to the echo. When they had viewed the site, charging about it in a ragged group like footballers without a ball, they scampered back to the bus screaming ecstatically. All aboard, we set off at breakneck speed through the suddenly-fallen darkness towards the ultimate objective of the tour, treat of treats, the Brindavan Gardens, and the little scholars' exuberance rose even higher, breaking out in clapping and cheering whenever their master spoke, in a way that brought a smile of something like benignity to his face. I think I was ignored, but I may have been part of the joke. Nobody warned me what to expect of the Brindavan Gardens.

When we stopped, all those eager faces formed a triumphal alley for master and prefect to pass down the bus. We stepped out into a nightmare of vulgarity. All around us electronic music shuddered and boomed, crackling with faulty connections. The darkness was ripped to shreds by coloured lights; here fountains threw up their umbrellas of jewelled water, there cascades blazed with underwater bulbs; everywhere, on bridges and paths and concrete steps, people swarmed and screamed. This was the Krishnarajasara Dam Garden, a vast and garish carnival of lights and colours and falling water. 'The enchanting Brindavan Gardens [says the guide book] present a scene of sublime wonder and beauty, especially under coloured illumination at night.' It is a perfectly Indian conception, copied no doubt in many a rich man's compound as well as in the grounds of David's grandmother's house. I felt that to stand at this source was to have understood a mystery. The mother of all electric rock gardens was in front of me.

I don't think an Englishman can ever be quite sure he isn't being teased in India. That flash of the filleting knife from David's father ('lordly English', 'horrible natives') gave vent by way of mockery to the pressure he evidently felt. The blankness of booking clerks in face of simple inquiries, the allocation of the worst room in an empty hotel, the palming off on me of five-rupee notes which were on the point of disintegration, the habit of selling me a packet of Charminars with two cigarettes missing, and postage stamps with no glue (a favourite contractor's economy) – it was tempting to read all the Lilliputian pinpricks of an Indian day as a form of that popular colonial game, 'Let's Tease the Englishman'. The only exception seemed to be David. If David mocked me, then he did it inside his head, a knife-flash glimpsed in the glitter of his eyes.

Gentle persecution by teasing, if that's what it was, did not make life less pleasant at the Metropole in those days. I felt I had been a resident for weeks. Every day brought the ivory merchant on his bicycle with boxes of chessmen under his arm and fresh arguments on his lips. We would meet over a pot of tea in the garden and bargain like two wrestlers on the mat. I wanted two sets, one for myself and another as a present for David, who for some reason only had men carved coarsely from wood, unless he kept in reserve others more precious which he did not show me. I was offering the merchant sterling, cash. But of course I had no idea what his bottom price was, and the effect of bargaining, especially when an unofficial exchange rate for foreign currency enters the equation, is to make you uncertain of the true value of anything anyway. The pieces were beautifully made, and the more closely I examined them the more I admired their design and workmanship – each figure made to screw into its base with a delicately-cut thread, each knight handsomely carved in the form of tiger's head, the tiger of Mysore, instead of the conventional horse's head of the rest of the world. But were they really ivory? Or bone? I made an offer which reflected my mistrust, and pushed the boxes away indifferently when it was rejected. Carefully, having quietly set down his teacup on the tin table, the merchant packed them up and swung his bicycle out of its parking place, moaning and wagging his head as he pedalled away as if into eternal destitution. Both of us knew the final outcome, when the game to while away time was done.

Or I thought we did. Ritualising our relationship made me comfortable with it, and I assumed he too was content to bicycle and bargain. Surely his tales of woe and misfortune, of money owed and bankruptcy at hand, were the conventional pieces he moved about the board to tease and outwit the

Englishman? Self-convinced, I need not wonder if I was being cruelly mean to a desperate man. In many ways, none of them deliberately heartless, I constructed shelter for what might be called my conscience. I noticed the way beggar-children, as I walked by, mimicked hunger with a rub of the tummy and a quickly pulled face of tears, lapsing back into jokes with friends as soon as I had passed. I threw them a coin and forgot them. How else can you live, in India?

Cocooned in comfortable notions I strolled about Mysore enjoying the statues under stone canopies, the Jubilee Clocks, the pillared façades of town hall and hospital and university, and the dust raised in the sunlight by ambling bullock-carts and trotting rickshaws. It was a curious mixture, princely Mysore. There was the rubbish of Indian towns, but an unusual municipal wish for the rubbish not to be there, a wish expressed in dustbins standing on mounds of garbage. On their sides was printed 'Use Me', and inside them, using them indeed, the dogs fought for scraps.

The many palaces, naturally enough, were the chief pieces of stage scenery in the over-garnished little town. *A Guide to Mysore* told me: 'During the Dasarna, the palace will be illuminated in the night, which will make the onlooker feel like moving in a fairy-land. The Maharaja has always been maintaining the illustrious Bodyguards and up-to-date Auto garages and stables, which are well worth visiting, if time permits.' If I visited the Bodyguards, their lustre left no impression on me. Told that I must apply to the maharaja's palace office outside the palace gate for permission to enter, I found the office empty, the whole set of offices hot and still and empty, their doors standing open. But the soldiers guarding the gate accepted a few pence to open it. I entered a granite-walled compound of grass and baked mud overlooked by gilt-domed towers, a stillness within which shut out all sound of the town. Only the green country hills, at some distance, peeped over the wall. Was it in this isolation that the Rulers lived? Wherever I walked the Home Guard shouted at me from windows and doors but I got used to them and took no notice. Gaining confidence (and remembering the Faridkot soldiery), when a group of them barred my way I told them to open a door for me, and waited for it to be done just as if I never opened doors for myself. This too, like his way with hotel clerks, was a manner not mine but borrowed from David. In Rome, if you wish to be comfortable, do as the Romans do. My impersonation never quite worked: an outsider can only do as the Romans appear to do, and I never acquired the guide walking a few steps behind me, who always appeared in David's train like a salute of guns acknowledging his status.

But nothing disturbed my satisfaction with Mysore: it was my reassuring belief that everyone, from maharaja to beggar-child, from ivory merchant to palace guard, was happy with their part in the *opéra bouffe* which I believed myself to be watching from my tin table outside the Metropole.

Then rather an uncomfortable thing happened. On the steps of the palace a cheerful young man materialised in the role of beggar at my elbow and opened his fist to disclose what it concealed. His air of mystery made me look: in the creased hollow of his hand there lay a single bean, betel-juice red. He lifted the bean between long fingers and showed me that mounted upon it, like a crown on an orb, was a miniature elephant carved from ivory. That was not all. As I watched he drew forth the elephant from its cavity, like the stopper from a bottle, and shook out of the hollow bean a cascade of tiny ivory snowflakes into the hollow of his hand. I looked. Each flake was carved into the form of an elephant – minute, fragile, delicate, yet perfectly elephantine. 'One hundred elephants,' the young man said. It was a fascinating thing and I wanted it. 'A hundred? Nonsense!' I replied. Disbelief had become a habit. 'Yes,' he repeated, 'one hundred.' 'More like twenty. How much do you want for it?' I looked up from the alluring palm into his face. I had made a mistake, he was not a beggar. He smiled regretfully. 'There are one hundred, sir, but I am not selling.' He poured the slivers of ivory from his palm into the bean and pushed home the ivory stopper. There was dignity and con-descension in the smile on his sad young face, as though this was what they had told him to expect from the world. 'I am not selling,' he repeated, 'I am giving.' He pressed the red bean into my coarse English hand and was gone in the crowd.

One evening I set out for the railway station in a *shah pasand*. I had intended never to hail one of these pony cabs I'd seen creaking about the town with a sorry bag of bones between the shafts and a seventeen-stone boxwalla sprawled behind the driver, but Bob and Louise, an American couple who had turned up at the Metropole and were keen to reach Poona, had ordered an unspecified 'taxi' through the hotel clerk, and a couple of these miserable vehicles had filled the order. I'd never minded seeing my luggage on a human head jogging through the streets, but I felt ashamed of the weight of it – the weight of my unnecessary wardrobe – behind the broken-kneed little creature struggling to keep on its legs under the blows of its driver's whip. Added to my experience as I left Mysore were several lessons, and added to my baggage were both ivory chess-sets, for which I had paid without further bargaining the sum first asked by the ivory merchant as he had wheeled his bicycle into the Metropole garden that morning. I also had in my shirt pocket, safe in a matchbox, the marvellous red bean holding its secret. That matchbox, Tekka Wax Matches, I have by me now with the bean inside it. Occasionally, over the quar-ter-century since it was given to me, one of the children or I have drawn the elephant stopper, tipped the bean, and let the ivory herd stampede into view. We never count them. It is an article of faith that, though there seem to be only about fifty or sixty elephants, there are really one hundred.

The booking-clerk had raised expectations by talking of 'top hole accommodation on the Poona Mail' but what we found at Mysore station trampled our Western notions flat: the compart-ment was a hot and dirty box lined with four plastic-covered shelves. Bob took it on the chin. Louise said 'Oh my!' From their nomad encampment nearby a migrant labour force from the North, which had made itself comfortable on the platform – more comfortable than ourselves in our first-class sleeper – cooked over their little fires and watched us through Tartar eyes. We had no provisions, and the Poona Mail provided nothing. Seven Fantas was all Bob and I found by scouring the vast Victorian station, and the question of how to return the empty bottles, a matter which no bribe would make the storekeeper forget, kept us arguing on the carriage step as steam hissed and whistles blew. At last the green flag showed and the train crawled out into the hot Indian night.

I withdrew to a top shelf and lay doggo in the heat, listening to Bob and Louise get on each other's nerves. She blamed him for India: for heat, dirt, smuts, for people at every station trying to climb into our carriage and start cooking on the floor – for every way this train differed from an American train, Louise blamed Bob. He took it all, and tried to put India right for her. Up and down he hopped, adjusting lights and fans and windows. Finally it was the cockroaches which got us all off our shelves to fight a common enemy, the nibbling, crawling, tickling little slivers of the dark and dirt of the carriage. Both sides won: the roaches didn't alter their habits, and we learned that we had to put up with them. I dozed, disturbed regularly by incidents of travel. A man with a stethoscope climbed in at one station and claimed he was a medical man rushing to a case down the line, but Louise had Bob throw him out. Half-wakening I listened to the plangent voices of Indian vendors wailing 'Tea! Tea! Tea!' through the hiss of steam at our window; and then it was dawn, the sun hot the minute its rich rays struck and reddened the train.

In David and in Mr Goyle I had found thoughtful and imaginative guardians. But when I stepped off the Poona Mail at Londa, a wayside junction in the midst of a hill-forest, at half past four in the afternoon, I stepped outside anyone's care. 'A

European in India [I wrote on a scrap of paper at the time] is like Johnny-Head-in-Air because of all these sudden holes you step into.' The Panjim train had gone. I'd missed the bus. The only car in the village had gone to Belgaum. There was nowhere to eat and nowhere to stay. This was the hole I fell into off the Poona Mail.

But it was only a hole in my European expectations, and I only fell into Indian reality. The Londa car, for instance, sounded worth exploring. 'No, too much money for you,' said my porter, rolling his head. 'All the same I'd like to see it,' I persevered. 'Very good car. Belong my father.' Off we jogged, my luggage on his head, until we came to an oil-stained clearing behind a hut where the car evidently dwelt. Out came a smoothie Brahmin, sprinkling water on his hands, with a child, an infant. The car's motive and objective in leaving he didn't know, shrugging his shoulders over it like the owner of a runaway horse, and when it would be back was anybody's guess. My porter's parental claims for it were evidently false. Everything else became unclear, and I had myself and baggage delivered back to the station, somehow the only established fact in all Londa. The next train onwards to Panjim was due at 3.30 am, ten hours away. I put my luggage in the lockable cloakroom cupboard (the ticket issued by the station master for this service managed to incorporate 400 words of bureaucratese) and walked in the setting sun up and down the platform, which ended each way in jungle. The sun sank; the rails glittered and went out. I retired into the first-class waiting-room and read the notices on the walls. There were three. The first said 'Hot Water Supplied on Request. Fee 8 annas for 3 buckets. Apply Station Master.' A second said 'Walls Whitewashed 8.12.72.' But it was the third that made me ponder, a pregnant yet tentative statement which might have been formulated by Sri Aurobindo himself: 'Trains Running Late Are Liable to Make Up or Lose Some Time.' It was the sort of statement Mr Goyle would have been happy with.

You are rarely long alone in India, which suits the gregarious traveller. Though I was used to a crowd, and used to the raucousness of India, I was exasperated by the schoolboys of ten or twelve who filled the waiting-room and drummed on the table and quarrelled with each other over whose turn it was to try to break the tap. I went for the station master, who followed me back and stood looking in timidly at the waiting-room door. What was my complaint? Oh, I said, the noise, the destruction, the fact that these boys weren't waiting for a train and didn't have first-class tickets. Ah, he replied, turning away towards his sanctum, what I needed was the Complaints Book, available at certain hours, in which `to write down my complaints and have them submitted to an overseer later in the year. No (and here I seized him by the arm), what I wanted was him to use his authority to clear the waiting-room NOW, or it would be about himself that I would fill a page of the Complaints Book. Stock still as if my touch had petrified him he squeaked out that the Complaints Book could only accept complaints which he as station master gave the green light to – a green light which he would certainly withhold in my case – and that anyway the book was unavailable until next morning. I let him go.

Slowly the waiting-room cleared of its own accord of all the schoolboys except one, who read aloud to himself in Tamil until he fell asleep. There was a roorkee chair, very hard, with long armrests, and in this I read. By ten o'clock even the metal-topped table, across which scampered the cockroaches, looked enviably comfortable. I climbed onto it and stretched out, my head on Mr Goyle's bag. Oddly I wasn't bothered by hunger or headache or any of the minor ills which can spoil things when you're tired. I pulled my L.L.Bean cap over my eyes to keep out the neon, and slept.

About 2 am I woke and went outside. The dimlit platform, which I had left empty save for a leper lying against a wall, was now crowded with blanketed bodies, maybe 200 of them, all corpse-quiet and patient and very poor. This silent company had surrounded me while I slept. Who were they? From the booking-clerk I learned that they were all waiting for my train to Panjim. Indifferent towards me as towards them, he shrugged off the question of whether or not I'd get a place on the train. As we argued, I saw that a north-bound train was waiting, steam up, and in it I saw an empty sleeper. I bought a ticket to Miraj, recovered my baggage from the lockup, climbed aboard and on to a coal-dusty upper bunk, and fell asleep. Miraj would do as well as anywhere else for a destination on this odyssey.

Asleep on the wrong train I was carried north safely through the night. Though I hadn't yet realised it, my travels had taken the course proposed to me that evening in the ashram: 'You just walk out the door. India'll take care of you.' After David, after Mr Goyle, ever since I caught the bus to Bangalore, I had been in the hands of India – protesting at first, fighting to stick to European plans, I had at last given up trying to get at the Complaints Book to make India conform, and I'd got on the train to Miraj and fallen asleep. What good care India had taken of me. Never ill, never unhappy, never bored, I had had my plans replaced by serendipity. I left on Londa station baggage I have never gone back to claim, whose loss lightened me so that other more difficult journeys were made possible. 'Trains Running Late Are Liable to Make Up or Lose Some Time': I had absorbed the Londa Aphorism.

The literal truth of the aphorism was demonstrated by catching up with Bob eating Marie biscuits at the foodstall on Miraj station first thing next morning. They had reached the place last night aboard the Poona Mail, found all onward trains had already left, and had had to look for a room. 'How did that go?' I asked. 'Well, I guess it was okay for me,' said Bob. This morning they had first-class seats booked on the Bombay train. 'God knows where you'll end up,' I said. 'Why, Bombay I guess,' he replied, 'they can't miss Bombay.' For him, even in Miraj, the apparatus was still in place. For myself, I had the world at my feet. We parted company. After studying the trains which happened to be approaching the hour which the timetable suggested for their departure, I decided on Poona as my destination, and squeezed into the only seat, second-class, which could be found for me on the Poona train by other passengers signalling helpfully from windows. At ten o'clock or so the train pushed out into the heat of Maharashta, under a sun as hot and heavy as a brazen pot cooking in a fiery sky.

It was a landscape of red dust and occasional stony hills, their watercourses dry. Water, though short, was awfully wasted. I remember watching a little girl trying to turn off a tap left running by men from the train filling their water bottles, her efforts idly observed by the usual loafers, and I remember how the engineers watering the engine behaved with the hose like clowns washing the circus elephant. Yet in that province the previous monsoon had failed, bringing famine followed by cholera. My neighbour in the train, the Madrassi who told me these things, was immensely disdainful of country people and their landscape, let his eye fall in judgement where it might. I had not seen Asia at that time, and I was fascinated – by the harshness of it, by the occasional robed sentinel leaning on a staff under a thorn tree watching sheep, by the bullock-cart raising a plume of dust from a white road, by the presence of its history. These country roads (so my neighbour told me) were a scandal, for stone-breaking and road-making were so much overused as public works that villages were joined to each other by as many as five roads, and all schemes until 1991 (eighteen years away) were already completed. Where I saw for the first time an intriguing Eastern landscape, he saw only provocation laid out especially to annoy a crusty nature. It struck me that his strictures on a mischievous and idle peasantry might have fallen from the lips of a diehard Tory traveller through Ireland in the 1840s, where similar road schemes formed public works for famine relief; but I saw myself having to carry too much material up too many gradients before he could see the irony in the parallel. An apparently-shared language can be so misleading. Better listen and nod.

There were four men on each wooden bench in the open compartment and several clusters of families of women and children on the floor; respectable middle-class people, for most of them talked to each other in English, and the men wore the nylon shirts, and slacks and sandals, of the bourgeoisie. A shrivelled little chap sat next to me at first, quiet for hours, motionless too until he suddenly sprang up into the luggage rack overhead, where he unrolled his bedding and went to sleep. His place was taken by an elderly babu, very black, who played rummy against his peon on the opposite bench, upsetting the poor servant's game by crying out sharply every moment or two 'Play! Play! You must play kvickly.' I hated him. It was impossible to be indifferent about so many people at such close quarters, and I soon nursed a private opinion about each of them.

It seemed as the hours wore by that I had been travelling in an Indian train for most of my life. In a state of permanent transience I was perfectly content, perfectly comfortable. I read, and looked out of the window, and speculated about the neighbours. I felt that I was doing what a would-be novelist should do: absorbing information offered about the human race; learning its actions and its attitudes as evidence of its multifarious characteristics; listening, watching, storing; profiting as readily from the chance that puts you on a train to Sevenoaks or Samarkand. I soon noted that the common denominator amongst passengers on the Poona train was a poor digestion. Every man, woman and child visited the toilet frequently, some as many as ten times in the seven hours of the journey. Indeed the toilet was never empty, never, and it was not a spot to pass time in for pleasure, though one mother, having cooked and served a meal of boiled rice to her family on the compartment floor, did her washing up in the toilet hand-basin in a very free and easy manner. Food for those without a woman to cook for them appeared in the form of curries brought aboard now and again by active little boys who stayed on the train till the next stop, gathering the empty dishes to clean them with eager fin-

gers of every leftover speck. Their place in society was the
bottom rung: they were obliged to sit on the step outside the
door and accept abuse from everyone. Thus with bullying and
cooking and eating and sleeping the passengers passed the time.
I left them about five o'clock, when the train threaded its way
through vast marshalling yards to stop in Poona station.

The moment the inanition of the journey was over, and I was
out of the train, anxieties returned. I knew from Fodor that
there was in Poona one 'first-class superior' hotel, the Blue
Diamond. Memorable hotels in my travels have, as I've said,
been those with more eccentricity than stars, but hotels with
eccentric character require energy to enjoy them, and from
Poona what I wanted was all the room service I could get.
What I most desired of the world, as my motor-rickshaw carried me along the sun-burnt road from the station, was for the
shining castle of concrete and glass which rose above the palms
and tin roofs ahead – the Blue Diamond – to contain an empty
room. Just one, please. *Please.*

Ten

The Blue Diamond's interior looked like Paradise. Aware of the air-conditioning, aware of the liquid whisper of a swimming-pool somewhere in the pillared marble shadows behind me, I stood at the desk waiting to be chosen or rejected. The clerk's pencil made a tick on his register, a key was issued to one of the now-eager bearers, my suitcase was lifted by another, and I followed the procession of angels through cool halls to an elevator. I was in. No matter that I might have passed the Blue Diamond with contempt in another country at another time: this was Poona, now, and I was in. The elevator mounted with a sigh towards heaven.

I never took more pleasure in being tired and dirty and hungry than I took when left alone in that modern room with the means at hand to satisfy all wants. Its window was shuttered against the sun; the air-conditioning purred. No need here, in a hotel of identical rooms, for a Khetri House inquiry. First I stripped and made my clothes into a bundle for laundry. From room service I ordered an omelette and two Fantas. As pants the hart I stepped into the shower and washed under a cascade of cold water. I ate the omelette, drank the Fantas. Then I repeated the recipe: another omelette, two more Fantas, a second shower. Immensely sleepy (though it was only mid-afternoon) I stood smiling face to face with my image in the bathroom mirror, as if we were companions reunited after adventures apart. Then I unfurled between clean sheets and slept.

The pleasures of arrival do not last, and it is the pleasures of arrival which hotels like the Blue Diamond are good at. The foyer promises more than the rest of the building can deliver.

Pretty soon the swimming-pool, the coffee shop, even room service – all the delectable components of welcome – begin to pall, while the air-conditioning creates round you a *cordon sanitaire* which has had all the Indian components, the scent and heat of India, washed out of it. You feel walled off from place and people. I missed the sense of belonging which my tin table outside the Metropole had fostered in Mysore. Under the drizzling muzak of the Blue Diamond's coffee shop I even found myself missing the Indianness of the Londa waiting-room. And compared to the people with whom I had shared the train from Miraj, or the bus from Pondicherry, I didn't find much to make me curious in the people togged out in swimsuits round the Blue Diamond pool.

One night was enough. I didn't need a rest from India, the way you pine for respite from the hostility of unfriendly countries. What exhausts mind and body in travels over hostile ground is the need to make up your life as you go along because it has no continuity of itself: you have to cut the next footstep, bridge the next chasm, contrive to hook this minute to the next, if you are to cross the unmapped country ahead, where the basic expectations of your own daily life are not in place. It's all pedalling uphill, no free-wheeling. I once went on my own in Soviet times to the Caucasus, having pressed in advance all the buttons offered by Intourist in London – self-drive car, pre-booked hotels, pre-arranged route – just as if I were planning to tour Wales. The arrangements made in London did not touch Soviet reality at any point. I had my hire-car but there was a petrol crisis, my booking but no room, my table but no food, my approved route but no map, roads but no signposts. I remember losing my way at dusk in the merciless traffic somewhere between Ordzhonikidze and Pyatigorsk – short of petrol, no means of knowing where I had gone wrong – with a sense of going down the plughole, panic, very unlike the sense of romantic isolation which I'd enjoyed at distant points on travels through terrain where the basic framework, however rusty, was in place. In the Caucasus it was not.

India was by no means hostile. India had taken every care of me, once I gave it the chance. Refreshed by all the Blue Diamond had to offer, yet anxious to widen my horizons, I stepped out next morning to stroll into central Poona.

But where *was* Poona, let alone central Poona? The hotel stood by itself, an alien tower of concrete and glass in a waste of dust and tenements. I strolled and strolled, but came upon no busy street or lively shops. It all seemed to be suburbs. I stopped a stray rickshaw and asked him to take me to Main Street. He looked puzzled. 'Empress Gardens?' he suggested. That sounded central, so I got in and was carried away. We passed through battered streets of two-storey brick houses barely better than slums. Queen Alexandra Road, Cantonment Lines – they led nowhere, just into more roads as featureless and peripheral as themselves. Set down at Empress Gardens, I found myself in as dull and dirty a little park as I ever saw. My rickshaw walla had vanished, no doubt to his home nearby. I was obliged to walk in the heat of the shadeless roads, navigating by the sun and the advice of passers-by. I crossed open ground, passed a burnt-grass racecourse, walked through an army camp. Where was Main Street? Nobody knew.

I know now, by light of much experience as the lost foreigner looking for Main Street, that I was looking not so much for the centre of Poona as for the point of Poona – its point for me. You can wander for hours in featureless streets, turn a corner and find yourself enchanted. On my trip to the Caucasus I remember driving into Kutais and becoming lost at once in a maze of one-way streets threaded between high-rise concrete. Twice, three times I drove round this conundrum and almost drove off in despair. Catching sight of one small arrowed sign saying CENTRE I parked where I was and walked. Nothing, nothing. Suddenly I turned a corner and found myself in the midst of all I'd hoped for – an old town, a provincial capital on the banks of a rapid river, fine shady streets of cut limestone façades, town houses dignified by pilasters, door cases, rusticated quoins. Spanning the Rion were stone bridges (mended with rusty Soviet girders) which led into steep lanes of cottages with figs and apples hanging ripe over garden walls. Below, the Rion flowed in spate over limestone rocks; over forested mountains the sun glowed through mist. Only by finding myself in the midst of the scene had I discovered in myself what I was looking for: authenticity, to see what I had only read about, to find the landscape which would support a novel set partly amongst those mountains in the 1860s. By turning a street corner in Kutais I had found it.

You have to know what you need specifically enough to recognise it when you see it. When I went to the Caucasus my novel was already drafted. In Poona fifteen years earlier my objective – settings for stories I hadn't even roughed out, let alone drafted – was too vague to be recognised, even if found. 'Atmosphere' is an elusive gas. But I wandered expectantly, and turned corners hopefully. You never know. Passing a pair of iron gates I turned in to a shady garden for a rest under the trees.

Immediately my foot crunched on gravel, an attendant in uniform bounced out of hiding and asked me my business, rapping with his cane a notice saying 'Botanical Museum'. Perhaps I overdid my interest in India's trees. I looked grave and said I had come far to add these famed gardens to my studies. Kew may have been mentioned as my HQ. For further screening he shepherded me inside the nearby building, an old stone villa, where I explained to an audience of curious clerks gazing up from their desks like penned lambs that I simply wanted a half-hour with their trees. The gatekeeper, peaked hat in hand, tramped off upstairs to seek a higher authority than existed here below. Silently the clerks looked up from paperwork hoping for a scene, violent if possible. When the gatekeeper returned he was following downstairs a thin young man putting on the jacket of a suit. He grasped my hands, we exchanged names, he held open the door. A path under the trees was indicated and we set off. The clerks went back to their books.

The young man from upstairs had been sent as my guide by order of someone important to him; he responded, not to me but to the hierarchical position which this order had allocated to me, and was obsequious. He walked a pace or two behind me, just as David's cicerones always did, and I understood that it wasn't David's personal haughtiness which made his guides drop back, it was in order to take up their proper place in the social procession. His deference meant I had trouble hearing what he said, but when I stopped for him to catch up, he stopped too, as if invisible buffers separated us. 'What is your work at Kew?' he called across one of these abysses. 'Oh, I don't work at Kew,' I called back thoughtlessly, 'I'm just interested in trees.' I walked on, and he followed. But it was not enough to be an amateur, with an amateur's interest, if I wanted respect in the botanical world this young Indian lived in. He kept his distance, but I felt now that the space between us represented his disdain not his respect. I was a fraud. He offered no information, answering my questions with the tree's Latin name only. By the time I left Poona's Botanical Gardens I had learned more about India than about India's trees.

Once fairly sure you can trust a country you come rather to rely on wrong turnings to show you what's interesting and unusual. With this serendipity you never accuse yourself (as a travelling companion would be sure to accuse you) of wasting time. A few days later, in Bombay, in an attempt to replace my wanderings in Poona with purposeful sightseeing, I booked myself a Bombay Highlights City Tour, and boarded the tour bus when it arrived at an early hour outside the Taj Hotel. We were under way before our tour leader, a lady, rose to welcome us, her opening remarks showing me that something was wrong. We – myself, three Filippinos and a German – were bound, not for Bombay Highlights, but for the Aerey Milk Colony. The expedition was in the charge of this roguish lady who sang rather than spoke into a mike clasped to bust and lips in crooner style. Her song was a paean to India's modernity. The bus rattled through residential Bombay, and past Chowpatty's beaches and sun-umbrellas, to emerge from the city onto the filth and ooze of mudflats – and still she warbled of other things, always repeating her refrain; 'You see, we are not at all a backward nation.' What we saw from the bus window became every minute more distressing. Beyond the mudflats we entered a slum city. 'We sell isotopes', she chirruped, 'to many first-world countries.' Hopeless rickety lanes of petrol-can shanties were divided by drains in which black naked children crawled like maggots in putrid wounds and women stooped to pick unspeakable verdure. Still our guide sang her hymn to another India, as if to charm away the India we saw, until, when the stench of death and disease had so invaded our bus that even the Filippinos pressed handkerchiefs to their noses, she trilled one line, 'Slum on your left', without herself giving the slum even the single glance which might have allowed it into her head.

Very soon, too soon if you worry about where your milk comes from, we reached Aerey Milk Colony, a pasteurising plant, its extensive buildings heavily protected by gates and wire. Inside the gates, a fortune had been spent on flowers. Further crores of Government rupees had erected an imposing Research Institute, already surrounded by the huts of expansionism. Research! It was the most seductive aspect of a project meant to be practical, as preferable to humdrum pasteurising as are isotopes to slums.

If I had stepped ashore that morning from a cruise ship, and seen as my first sight of India that slum Gehenna at the foot of a hill crowned by sleek researchers amongst their flowers, I would have been indignant at the want of charity and want of conscience – the false values – in an authority which tolerates it. But Indians are not ashamed of it: if they were, they would route the tourist bus differently. I think they are not ashamed – or were not at that time ashamed – because of the non-linear way in which the Indian mind views history. No part of the past is over: every age co-exists in the present, the way the transport of different centuries occupies the Grand Trunk Road together. Of course sections of the poor live an old-fashioned life-style. If you fail in India, you find yourself in the fourteenth century. There is no urge in an Indian's mind to bring everything up to date together. It doesn't matter which comes first, the cart or the horse. Isotopes and slums: they are not the outrageous moral collision to an Indian that they are to a Westerner newly landed from his cruise ship on the Apollo Bunder Pier; they merely exemplify the multifarious contemporaneity of Indian civilisation.

I didn't stay in the Taj Mahal Hotel – was it full or was I reacting against the Blue Diamond? – so when the Milk Colony tour dropped me at its door I took the opportunity to step in for lunch. It is marvellously sited. When I had walked to it in the early morning to catch the bus I had been much struck by the broad cool streets of magnificent imperial buildings leading to the waterfront – and then, in its clearing, the lost might of the Gateway to India outlined ponderous and forlorn against a misty sea creeping with sails. Right there, right opposite the Gateway, its decorated and many-windowed façade brightened by the rising sun, stands the Taj Hotel, first or last point of contact with India to so many travellers who had passed, or would pass, through the arch; terminus to many more. Its interior, its want of atmosphere, was a disappointment. No cabin trunks or gun cases or hat boxes waiting heaped together in the foyer. Just a busy nondescript crowd hurrying in and out, type of the travelling businessman, each looking for his car and for his driver, whose name a secretary had noted down in Berlin or Tokyo so that her boss could add his mite to international concord with a personalised 'Good morning, Abdul'. Through processing this crowd hotel staff become like operatives pushing sustenance into battery hens. Too efficient in its new role, too well known in business circles, and an erstwhile Grand Hotel loses its hauteur in the bustle of the business community and the luxury tour groups which will take it over and marginalise the private traveller. The perfect Grand Hotel (which I have never found) needs to be just in decline from former splendour, not so steeply that rats run over the serving tables in its dining-hall, but sufficiently off its peak for the suspicion of rats to be behind that shiver in the brocade curtain, that toothmark in the gesso, those droppings on the Turkey carpet. Temperamental electricity, eccentric servants, plumbing which regurgitates horrors – the businessman has not the energy for all this and goes instead for the Blue Diamond.

One of the objectives that took me into the Taj for lunch was to visit its shops, quite a little indoor street of them handy for guests who would rather not leave the hotel premises, so that I could compare prices with those in outside shops. I was looking for a piece of old ivory, a carving. Wherever I had been I had entered every shop I'd passed which appeared to sell antiques. What foggy ideas of the antique I met with. As with their history, so with their artefacts: Indians do not seem to share the European need to formalise the past into periods separate from one another and parcelled out in the datable segments of a linked historical process – Primitive, Renaissance, Baroque, Rococo – a hundred labels which distinguish one period from another and which, by making an index, keep the history of Western art in order. In India, just as there is little apparent development between the miniature paintings of the sixteenth to nineteenth centuries, so the necessity to allocate a work of art to a particular period is not felt. 'How old would you say this is?' I might ask the shopkeeper as I handled a reddish-tinged bottle carved from a huge tusk, which I guessed was probably nineteenth century and Burmese. 'Oh, sir, this is very old. It is thirty years old – or seventy?' He looked anxiously into my face. What age, he asked himself, did I want it to be? It was as though in dealing with stratified time he was quite out of his depth, his only concern that the object should be of an age which would persuade me to buy it.

It interested me to look for old ivories under these Oriental rules. Everything about Bombay interested me, and I did little enough, only wander about. That way your memory accumulates impressions without feeling force-fed. So often it is what you see by accident which is memorable. Once you appreciate this, the fluster of making plans you can't stick to may be forgotten. I had arrived in Bombay with my usual confusion, pushing out of the train from Poona with a thousand others only to realise too late that the station was a Bombay suburb, two stops before Victoria Terminal. Thank goodness I wasn't Bob, with Louise on my neck to bite me in the ear. It didn't matter: I waited for the next train, and watched the Indian world go by. On the platform across the tracks a spectacular Dickensian drunk, collar awry and hat on the back of his head, reeled through the crowd, clutching at passers-by and singing as he went, happy enough, and amusing the Bombay rush hour until he clutched the wrong man, who angrily shook off his hand and shoved him away; whereupon he fell flat as a tree-trunk, his song suddenly silenced like a bird killed in the tree's fall. There he lay, the crowd parting to hurry past him, until, flung by no particular hand, there flew a pailful of water which glistened through the lamplight and fell with a lovely crowd-scattering smack on his senseless form. It was most satisfactory. Would he stir? Before I could see how the scene across the tracks would develop, an incoming locomotive drew the curtain across it. Into the train I was crammed by the crush behind me, like a letter into a pigeon-hole, to have another shot at reaching the Victoria Terminal.

The Chinese monk Fa-hien travelled across India from Peshawar to the Hooghly between AD 399 and 414; travelled, that's to say, through the breadth of the Gupta empire about which (as usual with Indian history) little is reliably known and much is conjectured. Fa-hien had the opportunity to make for himself, merely by observing and recording what he saw, a name as famous as that of Pausanias or Marco Polo or the Abbé Huc. But he noticed nothing. He was not a wandering novelist like Graham Greene, an itinerant observer like Somerset Maugham; nor was he a gatherer of information like so many of the nineteenth-century travellers who mapped the world: Fa-hien was a pilgrim, and he noticed nothing unnecessary to that objective. Historians have wrung their hands over his tunnel vision ever since. Fa-hien came to India to visit the Buddhist holy places and to obtain authentic copies of the scriptures; he made his journey for the improvement of his soul, and looked neither to left or right of the pilgrim path. 'He had [and you can hear the sigh in the historian's words] ample opportunities for observing the life of northern India, but, unfortunately for posterity, his concentration on the object of his search seems to have left him little inclination to record his observations on secular matters, and he is silent regarding much that we desire to know.' I picture him embarking on the Hooghly river for Ceylon and home, smiling contentedly to himself at having laid eyes on the holy places, aware of increased wisdom, and grasping with satisfaction the bag containing the authentic scriptures. Authentic scriptures! What journey could produce more?

Restlessness, unknown to the pilgrim with his steady onward pace, is a disease fatal to the ordinary traveller's contentment. I had an air ticket, Bombay-Delhi, but I wanted to go next to Ahmedabad. When I found that Air India wouldn't re-route me I lost my enthusiasm for Ahmedabad. The thought of a flight direct to Delhi had been put into my mind in the cool Air India office and it stayed with me in the heat and clamour of Bombay. One evening I rang David. 'My dear Philip, no problem. Just turn up, your room is waiting.' I no sooner heard his voice clipping out the formal phrases than I half-regretted ringing him. Another reality, not in my own hands, waited for me in Delhi. My own private journey was over, my haphazard travels. India, teacher and nurse, had taken good care of me. And I had seen the electric rock garden.

Eleven

I lay in bed the first morning of my return to Jorbagh and listened to David's voice cry out for Massih's help in the exertion of beginning another day. The household sailed on. The arrival of bed-tea in my quiet cool little room reminded me that I had rejoined the ship, and that the customary programme lay ahead.

Jorbagh seemed like home. Later I strolled out to find the light misty, the sun wan, the air wintry. It was like England. How can this same North Indian maidan have seemed so hot and brilliant the morning I had arrived from London? How can I ever have thought it ramshackle and Oriental, this square, this greenery, these bird-chattering trees shading the trim little Jorbagh market? David appeared, bathed and scented, with much to discuss in the matter of Diana, who was for the moment absent from Delhi. The loafing life went on. We pottered and sat, and chatted and smoked, and the day passed.

I had been aware the previous night, as the airport bus carried me into town, of the un-Indianness of New Delhi. The place India – the vivid idea of India which had been scorched into my head by the branding-iron of the Southern sun – had vanished behind green avenues looking cold and deserted in the dark. From Connaught Place where the bus dropped me I took a Sikh-driven rickshaw and nearly froze on the road to Jorbagh. As I paid the driver, David toddled down his garden path, broad of beam, turbanless, domestic, welcoming.

'Where is your taxi? You surely have not come from Palam in a rickshaw?'

'I came in a bus.'

'Atcha! We must curry you out of this bus habit. Come along in and Massih will bring your traps.'

In we went. Whisky was poured for me, his own tumbler 'freshened', the needle of the gramophone reset. 'Now, my dear fellow, let me tell you...' She had arrived. She had offered to buy a house in England for their use (if married) for three months in the year. 'What do you say?' he inquired. I expressed my reservations. 'Mm...' He twisted his beard. 'I still don't quite fancy the idea.' So we chatted and sipped till two o'clock, and by bedtime it seemed I had never been away for a minute out of David's reach in the South. The India of my own discovery dimmed and faded.

I was careful not to dwell on my travels or to pontificate to David about his own country. For David's peace of mind my experiences had to agree with his picture of the India all foreigners are shown. A day or two after my return to Delhi he took me to a party given in Golf Links Colony for a couple from Texas who outlined the tour which their travel agent had devised to show them everything in India they could see in the meagre five days they could spare from the business which had brought them to the East. Five days! I could spend five days missing trains. Discussing their project when they had left the party David fished up one of the curious arguments which swam about in his head. In the long ago, he said, a visit to India took up a lot of time and money, so that to justify his outlay the traveller from the West must be parched by India's sun, threatened by her diseases, bitten by her snakes, swamped by her deluges and gnawed by her tigers. 'This cannot be managed in five days,' he concluded, 'and anyway too many people have seen on their quick tour that there are no snakes and diseases and therefore nothing true in the old stories the visitors were telling.'

'But, David, the Texan trawl is specially planned to avoid snakes and diseases.'

'Exactly my point. They see none, there are none.' The rusty cannon of his logic swung onto me and fired. 'Five days, five weeks. How many snakes did you see?' Boom! No traveller's tales from you, please, after your treacherous five weeks delving about behind my back to discover what I have not chosen to show you.

As I say, I guarded against the temptation to tell him things about India I thought he didn't know, but all the same I was watched for lapses from Delhi standards and nudged back into line if I showed signs of going native. When I suggested lunch at the Intercontinental (we were shopping nearby) he just touched his tie and murmured 'I think not...a tie needed.'

I suppose in the South I had dressed entirely for comfort, I scarcely recollect how, except that I remember wearing my pyjamas both indoors and out a good deal of the time. David, asked before I left for Madras what clothes I should need, had shuffled his shoes the way he did if invited into territory he wasn't sure of, or didn't approve as a subject of conversation, and replied testily, 'Oh, a few bush shirts I imagine.'

Bush shirts? By 1973 surely even the Army & Navy Stores had taken out of their window their last display of those much-gusseted semi-military garments which the old-timer in the East wore outside his tremendous shorts...though I'm not sure I don't recall David himself wearing such an item (freshly pressed and laundered like all his clothes) on our tour to Italy in days of youth and empire. In Delhi I wore a tweed change coat or a suit, depending on our engagements, following his lead. That was during the day. Evening parties – and there was a party of some sort every evening – were graded from buffets through 'sit-downs' to 'dee-jays', and for these last tip-top events I had brought from England a dinner-jacket (black, on David's advice, white being rather a gaffe in the Delhi cold-weather).

Chiefly it was the *corps diplomatique* which sat down and dressed up for its dinner, and into the diplomatic social world we went a great deal. Diplomats and their sanitised environment suited David. I often pondered his failure to pass the entrance exam into the Indian Foreign Office, but I never brought up the subject – failure was not a topic between us, though for each it was perhaps a spectre which hovered over the other's head. Yet to have judged from the number of ambassadors who asked him to dinner, one would have concluded that he was indeed a diplomat, and a rising star withal. That he wasn't, that he was sorely jealous of success, he showed by his disparagement of any of his friends whom I praised or admired. Our host one evening, in appearance a grand Indian, lived in an airy house in West End Colony with aquarium-like windows looking into the jungle greenery of a veranda furnished in marble and glass. He buttonholed me. Tipsier and tipsier he became, and more and more anxious to impress upon me that he knew the West End of London better than I did, enumerating for instance all the shirtmakers' shops on the south side of Jermyn Street. Via shirtmakers we talked of fishing shops. I let him know I remembered Ogden Smith's shop in St James's Street, and Carter's in South Molton Street, both of which he had forgotten. He faltered, distrust, even dislike, narrowing the bloodshot eyes he turned on me. Silent deference is the rule: never contest the top-sawyer's position. David's father was just the same. I stuck it well, and when David came over to see that I was cared for – nobody could have been more constantly watchful in that way – our host thrust his arm through mine and said 'David, when our friend comes again he will come fishing to Srinagar…no question of expense, all paid for.' As David and I walked off he told me that the man's ancestors had piled together an immense fortune by fiddling the commissariat of the British Army during the Afghan Wars, that he had brought £1 million out of Lahore at the time of Partition, and had now spent the lot. 'No chance of him paying for you in Kashmir,' he concluded with satisfaction. Had rich or ruling-class Indians always rejoiced in the calamity of one of their fellows, or was it a failing brought about by conditions post-Partition, which threatened them all? I remembered David's granny, at Faridkot, smacking her lips over a neighbour forced to sell up. 'I may try to buy one of his clocks.' Her want of sophistication took the malice out of the remark, but the attitude was viperish.

The Indians met on David's circuit were not sophisticated; not, at any rate, in their leisure hours, which is when I saw them. An evening which took us to the Asoka Supper Club after a dinner party was further extended by a great bear of a man, a rich industrialist, who first attached his table to ours beside the dance floor and then swept us all up and carried us off to his Golf Links house 'for a bottle or two of my usual Pee-jay.' He was anxious that bubbly should seem to us his every-day drink, but anxious also that we should acknowledge a rare treat by making a fuss. The Perrier-Jouet was poured, glasses raised to flatter our host. In the party were three princes, a maharaja's daughter, several tycoons – and I think only David knew the beverage was not champagne at all, let alone 'Pee-jay'. At any rate he was the only one who didn't drink it. Whilst he discreetly set down his full glass one of the princes held out his empty one, saying 'Delicious, very good, give me more.' 'Not very good – EXCELLENT!' roared out our host, splashing a few drops more into the proffered glass, 'Pee-jay is THE BEST!'

Of course it has to be remembered that David was a full-time trifler, whilst these other men (two were MPs and the rest of the party were industrialists or businessmen) kept the world of tri-fles for their recreation. You can't judge a man's worth by seeing him only at leisure – unless, like David, he is always at leisure. In an English restaurant, and on our European travels together, I had thought it a rather a boring and naïve character-istic of David's that he recited the names of the rarest clarets, and chatted with the sommelier, and sniffed the cork. In Delhi I saw how uncommon such knowledge was, though pretended to by many.

Strange, and contradictory, that such arcane knowledge – the shirtmakers in Jermyn Street, the best years of Pichon-Longueville – conferred status among Anglicised Indians who scoffed at Britain's true claims to greatness, past and present, and were quick to deride the Englishmen who served them best. I heard David replying to a friend who had told him of two retired British officers of a Sikh regiment who had been flown out to Delhi for a reunion: 'Must be a pretty good surprise for them,' he said, 'whipped out of their little council house or whatever and treated to a couple of ADCs running about. Give them something to boast about in the pub.' Just the same disparagement showed itself later that year, when David was staying with us and we had dined with a Dorset neighbour whose military career had taken him to India. This retired colonel's politeness about India, and his stories recalling enjoyment of Indian life, were taken by David to mean that the poor old soldier had never been content with England after his hour of grandeur at India's charge. It was an *idée fixe* with him. In vain we pointed out that this 'poor old soldier' lived with his family comfortably and farmed his own land, with enough money to shoot and hunt as well as to add to a notable collection of pictures. No use: David had spat his venom on the colonel, and would not alter his view. Possibly I had missed a piece of swordplay between them on some Indian matter in which David's self-esteem had been assailed. Of his self-esteem – his standing in his own eyes and in the eyes of the world – David was watchful and jealous.

This vigilance to preserve his standing is a vital instinct in an Oriental. In certain families it is no more than a couple of generations since his life would have depended on it – depended on his quickness in perceiving the withdrawal of respect by his courtiers which gave the ruler a brief warning of conspiracy and the assassin's knife. 'In this unhappy family [wrote the historian of Faridkot] it was the exception not the rule for death to result from natural causes.' David watched his back. He kept his cousin Michael under surveillance. His sharp eye had noticed Mme Hotz, in Agra, had put on her jewellery to meet him. I remembered his father growling to himself as the birthday guests arrived, 'In Faridkot also they wash behind their ears when you ask them to dine.' In Delhi David took me one

evening for a 'duty-drink' with a policeman who for some purpose was to be flattered. The officer, a huge Sikh, lived in a government house with his family, all of them on parade with three
or four other guests, the atmosphere constrained and our host
unctuous. David sniffed the silence – the awkwardness, the
constraint – and its tribute pleased him, like a god sniffing the
smoke of sacrifices. Led to a chair he sat down, accepted
whisky, chatted amiably. When we came away he said, 'Scotch
for us, you notice. Indian beer for his chums.' Distasteful to
English ears, but in India a sign that the social order is in place.
In Rome, in Trastevere, my neighbour (with whom I shared a
small garden) was a respectable printer who, when he asked me
to lunch, served me my food without eating himself, whilst his
old wife appeared only for a moment to curtsy from the kitchen
door. I felt uncomfortable, a fraud; but they had allotted me a
place in the order of things so as not to feel uncomfortable
themselves, and with their hospitality my sense of awkwardness was quickly overcome. It is insular to judge always by
your own standards. David's servants didn't, by English standards, live well in his garage; but by Delhi standards they did,
and I don't think they complained, or thought their master
harsh, any more than his mother's gatekeeper thought David
unkind when he hooted for entry in the middle of the night –
we were taking Her Highness home after a party – and drove in
through the opened gateway without acknowledging by the
least sign that a human soul stood bowing at its side. In America you press a button and the gate opens; in India you press
your horn.

David's mother lived in a house, and indeed led a life, which
made you expect crazy paving in her garden and gnomes
angling by her pool. The house was brick, 1930ish, with big
plain rooms and shiny sofas, in the midst of which comforts
Her Highness – separated from David's father – gave the
impression of a large purring soft-furred cat, with paws tucked
under her and a bowl of cream at hand – a contrasting line in
David's ancestry from the Sikh warlords of the Punjab. I think

she had little domestic control over David, but maybe she had influence, and I saw what she tried to be to him, or hoped to provide, the first time we met. Having been picked up by David and me from her twice-weekly bridge afternoon at the Gymkhana – if she had learned her bridge at Faridkot I was sorry for her partners – she noticed a button missing from David's suit and, in consequence, insisted on us coming into her house for repairs. There was a drinks trolley in the lounge, a large-wheeled affair in brass and teak, at which David poured us all whisky whilst a bell brought a servant who was despatched for a sewing-box. This girl did not sew on the button; when Her Highness had been fixed up with a threaded needle, the button, the jacket, and her spectacles, she performed the motherly task herself, afterwards helping David into his jacket as a priestess might invest her champion with raiment woven for his safekeeping at her faery loom. I liked her. She had the habit, or gift, of talking intimately, and when we met elsewhere she revealed her worries over David's future. Believing as she did in petticoat power, it was whom he chose to marry that she thought mattered most. Was he going to marry this English lady? Was it sensible to 'marry foreign'. What did I think?

The lady in question, David's chief concern and talking point in the days after my return from Bombay, who had left Delhi on some errand, or to show her independence, was now expected back, a prospect viewed by David with uncomfortable excitement. Her shadow fell across the agreeable dawdle of our days. Take the day before her return, a Tuesday, washing-day in Jorbagh, when David's attendance with the laundry list was required to oversee Massih's meeting with the dhobi, a piece of business which delayed breakfast until a quarter to eleven. By the time we were bathed and dressed it was midday, so that to gain one result from the morning – to buy me as it happened a second suitcase in which to take home my acquisitions – meant haste and activity. 'Now,' said David, settling in his garden chair after lunch, and opening the silver *pan dan* which Massih always placed on the table when he had cleared it, 'let me see. What have we achieved in our busy morning? Oh yes – bought your suitcase. Somehow I don't feel quite like having the car serviced today. Sleep this afternoon I think.' He foresaw this sort of timetable coming to an end.

It was necessary to him that we should face Diana together, two drones shoulder to shoulder more respectable than one, my idleness explaining or ameliorating his. He would not have me dodging my responsibilities to him – my loyalty – by calling myself a novelist. If I did so, his eyes would veil over, and the subject would be changed. Before long he would return to it obliquely, clearing his throat to ask 'And how is the big novel about India going along?'

It was certainly a mystery to me how he had got in so deep with this person from England – he who had assessed his own wants so acutely by taking Leda as his consort at Cambridge and a married woman for his Delhi mistress – but I suppose his mistake resulted from the basic contempt, concealed under formal courtesy, which made him think that women were all alike, prostitutes no worse than princesses and no better. If he married Diana both he and his opinion would be corrected: nothing, none of the little structures he counted on, would remain standing. No wonder he twisted his beard and shuffled his shoes and was inattentive at chess – chess played now with the ivory men I had brought him from Mysore, a present he had accepted in the same off-hand manner I had encountered with his father, a tributary gift which acknowledges the donor's gratitude but by no means erases his debt.

The day of Diana's return was reached, a telephone to her hotel confirmed that no happy intervention had delayed her. Massih and the industrious Mug, urged on by David in dressing-gown and bobbing topknot, worked as never before to prepare the *dîner intime* whose outcome might destroy them all. I borrowed David's car and drove myself to the Intercontinental to dine alone.

I walked into David's sitting-room from his garden the morning after Diana's return to find a willowy young woman accepting a drink from Massih. She held out her hand. 'I am the Maharani of K...' She was fun. She was enthusiastic and feminine and charming, and used gender in her voice and manner so that talking with her was like flirting in an old-fashioned dizzy way. She told me we had ruined our Indian empire by bringing out the memsahibs to introduce abroad the snobberies and suburban habits of their own class at home, virtuous dullness in place of the reckless representatives of the Company, who had lived at the native courts in the style of the native rajas and had steered India's wealth into English coffers.

'Guys like the Frasers here in Delhi, you mean, and Whatshisname at Hyderabad,' put in an English voice behind me. Diana had joined the group. David introduced her to the maharani and to a colonel, the President's Deputy Military Secretary, who stood respectfully at hand. Me she had met earlier.

I watched her. Neat, assured, soignée, upswept hair a dark copper colour, she gave the impression of a first-rate p.a. promising to bring correctness and order out of chaos. Flirting ceased. Voices clashed high and excitedly as the old ground of the memsahibs' rule was argued over. Whatever these upper-class Indians said, it was the influence of middle-class memsahibs which had formed their society, not the example of earlier adventurers they professed to admire. The old raja's style of living was forgotten, even by the rajas, in favour of the cramped rules of the collector's bungalow. I was a visitor, my point of view an outsider's, but for Diana, as she listened to the maharani arguing with the colonel, the issue was serious. I watched her patting her hair-do thoughtfully. I wondered what she wrote in her diary.

A day or two later I was walking behind David and Diana on a trip into Old Delhi. On my account, under David's leadership, we were making for the street of silversmiths, and ahead of me the two of them powered through the crowd of people, scattering rickshaws and cattle like two liners steaming for port through a crowd of skiffs. I saw how the Indians turned and stared after them.

At his shop like a booth in a traders' khan, I was introduced to David's family silversmith as a lamb to the slaughter. After respectful greetings, and Fanta all round, business commenced. I certainly wanted silver – beakers, ashtrays, a water jug – but was cautious, off-hand. The silversmith was by turns tragic, bitter, indifferent and angry. As the contest progressed David changed sides, joined the shopkeeper's camp, urged me to spend lavishly ('Ten only? Have a dozen, just think what they would cost you in UK'). The merchant was infinitely pliable, pushing away what I rejected, calling to his assistant behind the curtain to bring out more and more examples of his craft, silver formed into many different styles and tastes, from the wrought intricacy of the Orient to plain English 'Georgian'. The ashtrays I liked had a silver rupee set in each base, but the rupees looked to me obvious forgeries rather than the genuine coins he and David claimed them to be. This scarcely mattered, but the question of his honesty counted for a great deal if I was to take up the offer he made me. To save me paying English import duty on whatever silver I bought from him, he suggested that none of it should be hallmarked, so that I could take it through Customs as 'white metal' and pay nothing. Well. If he saw that I was prepared to be dishonest with the Customs did I trust him to be honest with me – to turn down the chance to charge an Englishman for silver whilst palming him off with 'white metal'? No danger of me exposing the fraud: his certificate would state, truly, that what I had bought was not silver. A neat scam. David and his silversmith, Indians together allied, watched my avarice at war with my caution.

The threat of the mob, or of a jealous ruler, towards settled wealth has always kept the rich Indian on his toes, and formed his attitude towards possessions. What I bought in the Dariba that day (if the articles were indeed silver) was a temporary incarnation of bullion, the age-old stuff of wealth, so many troy ounces of precious metal which I could melt down and reincarnate in different forms as often as I liked, or, in bad times, could store by me as the melted-down essence of wealth which could be pocketed when the mob broke down the front door and I had to flee by the back. It is the temporary nature of the incarnation of his treasure which makes an Indian indifferent to the swell of a gold tankard or the curve of a silver jug. Precious metalwork a century or two old, abundant in Europe for middle-class everyday use, is rare in unsettled India. David's father's bullion, I know, was in a constant state of flux, now an ingot, now a table centrepiece, and the jewels his family owned would many of them have been unset, even uncut, a handful of rough emeralds and diamonds to be snatched up in a wash-leather bag and taken whither the storm drove, as the last Emir fled with his portable treasure from Bokhara when that city fell to the Bolsheviks. One of the tasks the thrifty paramountcy of the British set itself was to teach native Rulers not to keep their wealth heaped idly up in coin and gems and precious metal in a vault beneath a fortress, but to make money work, to separate income from capital and forget the love of hoarded treasure. Their trust in this policy, encouraged by the Pax Britannica, had been shattered by Partition, emergency, and war – as well as by Mrs Gandhi withholding the purses for which the princes had given up their revenues – so that the old ideas from uncertain times had been restored.

It was interesting to see these old ideas come into view in David's nature. One morning he had gone to see his grandmother, not the one I had met at Faridkot, but his mother's mother. Diana and I were waiting for him at Jorbagh for lunch. With a banging of doors and a bustle of feet he burst in, almost running, and threw down a bundle of money. 'Count it! Count it!' he cried, dabbing his beard from the haste with which he had dashed home through the heat to share with us the thrill of handling cash.

Diana counted the notes. He watched her keenly. 'Eleven

thousand?' 'Right,' she said flatly, adding the word 'Scrummy' in an effort to sound enthusiastic. David took up the bundle and counted the notes into stacks on the carpet. 'Eleven thousand rupees.' I looked at Diana. The king was in his counting-house. What could she be making of it?

I had supposed, at Cambridge, that David like most of us valued money for what it could be turned into without looking for satisfaction in the raw money itself. His outlook was more complex. He laid out his money to secure an effect, the effect of extravagance, without having sufficient funds really to be extravagant. He had to be careful while studying to look careless. It was the canny side of his nature in control of his romanticism. But only just in control; in his nature, in his heart, was a streak of recklessness older and deeper than his caution. It was what made him love gambling, revel in the atmosphere of casinos, crave to see wealth exhibited in the big chips on the table, shrug off losses, rejoice when tokens he won were turned into cash at the door. I had watched his increasing excitement in the Venice casino as he lost all the money to which he had access, obliging us to steal away from the Danieli in a midnight gondola and make haste to Switzerland, where further funds were available. Altogether the collection of ideas called gambling suited him, so that it was a great disappointment to him (which he hid most courteously at the time) to be excluded because he was not yet twenty-one from the casino at Aix-les-Bains in our Long Vacation trip together. He didn't give up hope that Italian rules would be less stringent, or its officials more amenable to a present, and within a day or so of reaching Florence, restless for entertainment after dinner, he suggested that we find out if there existed in the city a private gambling-house, as someone at a Fiesole dinner party had indicated that there did. David was a believer in the power and discreet knowledge vested in the head porter of a grand hotel, an index which might be tapped by wealth and swagger. Accordingly, though staying somewhere modest on my account, we dined next night at the Excelsior where David, attracting the usual favourable staff attention as we strolled out through the lobby, beckoned the head porter to him and asked for the address of this casino. Unsurprised, the man wrote down the number of a house in one of the streets off Via Tornabuoni and we walked out accompanied by his sidekicks into the square. Here was a difficulty. At the Fiesole dinner party the previous night there had been a charming Florentine girl who had wrapped David round her little finger, so that she had easily persuaded him, when we had ended up at her parents' house at three in the morning, to leave her his car for a few days in exchange for her Lambretta (which David, exclaiming how he loved scooters, had ridden back from Fiesole with her clasping his waist from the pillion and me at the wheel of the Bentley behind). All day we had been having fun with the Lambretta, which David had soon taught me to ride by shouting instructions in my ear from the pillion as we flashed down the Viale Michelangelo before dawn, but now, outside the Excelsior after dinner with an escort of porters, a dented scooter was our only transport. Money was distributed. Gravely David threw his leg over the saddle. I climbed on behind and off we went. Parking at a discreet distance from the casino we approached it on foot, rang a bell and were admitted into a scented and soft-lit house. Ushered by an elderly servant into a sort of parlour, with a tiled floor and a good deal of red velvet in its furnishing, we were left alone for a few minutes. Then a door opened and girls began to come into the parlour. In they came, smiling away, one after another until every seat was taken. Surely they couldn't all be croupiers? Blonde, brunette or redhead, some in their underclothes and some ready for bed, it was a dazzling sight for a couple of youngsters who had hoped only for a hand of blackjack. Instead we learned that in Italy there are two kinds of casino, one with an accent on the 'o' and the other without.

Twelve

How frankly David had shown his hand to Diana (or to me) I tried to gauge for myself from my seat behind them in the Ambassador travelling north on the Grand Trunk Road a few days later. We were en route for Simla. In front of me the pair chirruped and giggled, his turban cosying up to her hair-do like two birds on a perch. Above her frock satiny shoulders turned this way and that as she darted out questions. She belonged to the era of empires, David's era too. 'Cost' she pronounced 'caust', 'girl' as 'gel'. Is she angling for him, I wondered. He thought so – or wished it so out of pride, wanting to be fished for by a woman the world admired. Because her trip was 'causting' her £1,000, he believed she must be investing her grand with hopes of striking gold – the Faridkot millions. I thought it likely that she had made the trip so as to do something 'perfectly scrummy' to kick sand in her friends' faces, confiding by airmail that there was 'this darling prince mad to marry me'. Listening to their conversation from the back seat I noticed how frequently poor David seized hold of the stick by its wrong end – 'And David, would you say that Chandigarh had come off as a town?' 'Not at all, it is maintaining very high status' – and I noticed too how prudently and patiently Diana steered around such contretemps. Molehills now maybe, but how hard it would be to maintain such patience in the face of constant misunderstanding in the everyday talk of husband and wife. Had she the penetration that sees in advance which mole-hills are going to turn into mountains? You can make up your mind on the big issue – shall I marry an Indian? – and forget that in a marriage it is not the camel but the gnats that you have to keep on swallowing on a daily basis.

David, by no means a realist in most things, took an unvarnished view of his standing in England and of the loyalty, or want of it, among his 'friends'. Turning upon himself the same cynical heartlessness with which he viewed others, he considered that it was his position in the world, and that only – not his character or his nature – which attracted English people to him. That position, the wealthy prince, could not be sustained permanently in England. His British income sufficed, as I have said, for him to live as a prosperous visitor for two or three months every three years – so long as he let dividends accumulate in his absence – and he therefore confined himself to these triennial appearances. Cold-blooded cynicism persuaded him that an everyday Indian, a touch close with his cash, who lived constantly among them, would be 'quite another cup of tea' from the triennial meteorite. On his last visit someone had given a ball for him, another had entertained him in a country house full of servants, a third had taken him into a box for the Oaks. For the two or three months he was in England everyone pulled out the stops, particularly those whom he had entertained in India.

Conscious that I was now in the indebted category myself, I pondered what it would take to make David comfortable when he came to stay. Glenfiddich whisky, a radio in his room, early tea, the papers and someone to talk to over a late breakfast, an outing by car, a short walk on level ground, people to lunch or dinner, chess and ping-pong in the intervals, gin before lunch and whisky before dinner, plenty of claret at meals and a shower in his bathroom. That was my list, and it didn't look much in return for all he had provided for me.

In September of that same year he came to stay with us for a fortnight. His visit turned out to be full-time work for the whole household. His expectation, from the moment he came downstairs for breakfast carefully dressed in tweed coat, flannels and a tie – having invariably left the dirty water in his bath and never thinking it necessary to carry down his early-tea tray – was for a host with unlimited time to spend in his company.

He was inflexible. For the life he liked to lead, and expected to lead in Dorset as elsewhere, servants to perform every task were the same unspoken necessity as is their presence below stairs in the country houses Bertie Wooster stays in. Fires had to be laid, silver and glass looked after, rooms prepared, tables set for meals – all by the same host who was needed for the little level walks, the outings by car, the games of chess and ping-pong, the gin before lunch and the whisky before dinner. Was he aware of the pressure, amused by watching my difficulties, using his inflexibility to show up the inadequacies of my life in Dorset compared to his own in India? On me his visit meant wear and tear, but I had the fun of his company, which I loved; on the household his presence was an unmitigated burden. His formality, the polite condescension of his manners, his complacent monopolisation of my time, his want of interest in women and children – all of himself that he showed was bitterly resented. Perhaps that suited his humour. Since the birth of our son six months before, the pivot of the house, indeed the pivot of life altogether, had become the nursery. But when our game of chess was interrupted for me to bid the baby goodnight, I returned to David and the Mysore chessmen as if returning to what mattered after the tiresome intrusion of married life into our bachelor games. Billiards we played too, and in the amusement arcade at Lyme Regis we discovered an electronic ping-pong game played on a television screen, which David preferred to live ping-pong, so we frequently motored in the evening the ten or so miles to Lyme, stopping on our way home for a drink at some dead-and-alive country house hotel.

These country house hotels were a will o' the wisp beguiling David, an idea, or an ideal, which appealed to his nature more truly than the genuine country house they supposedly imitated – rather as he preferred electronic ping-pong (and an electric rock garden) to the real thing. No struggling up a mountain to view the natural cataract; he liked to press a button and have the fountains start playing. One evening, driving back as usual from Lyme Regis, he noticed a finger-post: 'Fair Haven Hotel,

Two Miles'. He twiddled the wheel, followed the lane. 'Let's see,' he said. Because of his interest I pictured something Anglo-Indian at journey's end, carved gables and wooden verandas, corridors smelling of curry, brass trays from Benares, a gong suspended between elephant's tusks, a breezy proprietor with a silk scarf round his neck – a version, in short, of the Anglicised India of the palace guest-house where we had lunched at Bharatpur, somewhere familiar and comfortable to David's divided nature, where he could ring bells for service and rest undisturbed between engagements. But we never found Fair Haven. At the lane's inevitable fork there was no signpost. Between high Devon hedges we followed each alternative, one deep lane leading us to the usual farmyard full of barking sheepdogs which awaits the lost traveller, the other narrowing into a grass-grown track. 'Stumped!' He turned the car with difficulty in a gateway, already too stout and stiff to look over his shoulder.

There was one ominous reason behind David's preference for a hotel to a private house: drink. I had no idea how much alcohol he was sinking until I came to supply it. Two gins before lunch and two whiskies before dinner, I had thought in India. It was all I was aware of; the host can 'freshen his glass' in private. In Dorset I learned the truth – that a bottle of gin and another of whisky lasted him a couple of days. Still the intake had no visible effect on him, no effect on his chess or his ping-pong, at either of which he could beat me in his stony style just before going to bed. 'Goodnight, my dear Philip, thank you so much for another charming day.' Laying down his bat, away upstairs he would steadily tread, leaving me to the clearing up when he had gone.

Behind his back in the Ambassador travelling north on the Grand Trunk Road I tried to imagine him married. David was so set in his ways and in his views. Like all men with a low opinion of women, his expectation of their bad behaviour caused him to be extremely jealous. Believing any woman could be bought, he was watchful of higher bidders than himself for his own 'escort'. In truth a straightforward commercial relationship probably suited him best, for he calculated that you possess only what you have paid for. Like Sidonia in *Coningsby* 'something of the old Oriental vein influenced him in his carriage towards women. He was oftener behind the scenes at the Opera House than in his box: he delighted, too, in the company of "hetairai"; Aspasia was his heroine.' The difficulty, the confusion, would have come if Sidonia had married Aspasia. Diana was of course no Aspasia, but her ordinary manner towards the male sex was roguish; she wanted to be noticed and liked, and she set about it frankly, encouraging men she had just met to tease and joke with her so that the chummy atmosphere was created in which she throve, voted by all a thoroughly good sort. David plainly did not like this; it was a mistake Aspasias did not make. A waspishness showed itself towards the Indians who clustered round Diana at parties. I heard him telling a large hirsute pipe-smoking Cambridge man, over-attentive to her at a reception in the Mexican embassy, 'You stick to insurance, that's what you sell isn't it?' His tone was distinctly huffy.

A hundred years before, a huffy tone in the mouth of a Sikh prince might have spelt unpleasant consequences for an intended bride. Not some remote medieval ancestor, but David's great-grandfather, could have had a woman smothered for less. Did Diana allow for the presence in David's blood of a Dark Age of tyranny and treachery, the past co-existing with the present in his veins like the bullock-cart with the Ambassador on the arterial Grand Trunk Road? Faridkot's nineteenth-century history, which I did not hear from David, was by no means all picnics. According to one of the indefatigable young officers scouting the Indian frontiers in the 1820s, a Captain Murray, the kingdom was then all sand and desert scrub; it was by siding with the British in the Sikh Wars, and again in the Mutiny, that the Rajas of 'Furreedkote' earned themselves an eleven-gun salute and grants which tripled their revenue. In the Sikh Wars the great Ranjit Singh had taken the fort (or had engineered its betrayal to him), but the peace terms took from him all his cis-Sutlej possessions, and Faridkot was handed back to its family of chiefs, who returned with new appetite to their habits of debauch and muder. It was 'the invariable rule', writes their historian, for son to take up arms against father in each generation. The murder at birth of female babies flourished here until a Mr Clarke, about 1840, thought he had ended it.

We had been together to a wedding in Delhi, which showed a Sikh marriage – like other Oriental matches – to be an agreement between two families, the bride and groom treated throughout like children. The vulgarity was fearsome, the whole house and garden (a Lutyens bungalow in Aurangzeb Road) spangled with electric bulbs and gushing with coloured fountains amid a throng of confabulating turbans whose owners all earnestly and tipsily tramped wedding food into the lawn. Imagine accepting the role of bride in that tableau. You'd need to be in love, or blind, or mighty adventurous to go through with it. Both Diana's eyes were open, that was certain. Observation of her jawline from the back seat assured me that she required no looking after.

Perhaps I was jealous. Relegated to the gooseberry role behind the love-birds, my judgement of Diana's character and intentions were spiteful. She maintained her good temper. Though I'm sure I exasperated her (in those days I took exasperation for the tribute of those defeated in argument), she didn't retaliate, her fighting-knife sheathed on account of our position as fellow guests. Or perhaps she was sensitive to her occupancy of the place she had taken up between David and myself. But that wasn't quite the point. It wasn't David's sole attention that I missed – not our strolls in the Lodi gardens, our chess under the sunshade, our leisurely discussion of the day's events over a last whisky and soda at night – so much as the agreeable personality David showed me when we were alone but obscured behind a cloak of formality when others were present. I missed the unguarded talk, the infectious giggle, which left open a door into that strange polyglot head. *That* had been the sightseeing which had intrigued and instructed me most in all India, my trips into David's head. Diana's presence had closed that door to me; in order, perhaps, to enter it herself.

It was a long drive to Simla, ten hours through the North India landscape, our route at Ambala leaving the Grand Trunk, which continues thence to Amritsar. I thought of saying something provocative about the Amritsar massacre of 1919, to see where Diana stood on imperial gestures – to see what compromise she and David could hit upon as a bridge over an Anglo-Indian contretemps – but I didn't. I felt too isolated to control such a conversation from my back seat. Besides, my own ideas were less decided after two months in India than when I had watched the Republic Day floats bearing their travesties (it had seemed to me) of historical events. The Amritsar massacre was an example of a sober event in British imperial history which had been painted into Indian mythology with the brush of poetic nationalism. Being in India, my experience of India, had shown me both points of view: it was an action justifiable in the context of running an empire, when that activity was morally unquestioned; and it was the kind of action a foreign tyrant carries out, the sort of incident which begs to be mythologised. The gunfire at Amritsar caught the ear of the post-1914 world as an echo of the bad old Victorian days. Dyer faced an inquiry which was in effect a trial, and as a result resigned the service. Meanwhile readers of the *Daily Post* contributed £20,000 as a testimonial to his character and his action, and India prepared for him a place in the permanent hellfire of being hanged in effigy on every float in the land. I saw the point of each view. I felt more and more like Mr Goyle.

In that long drive north there was Chandigarh, too, the big oblong secretariat and high court standing alone amid scrub, clerks strolling in pairs in black shoes in a waste of dust and rubbish; a lake urbanised by its esplanade on one side, petering out into reeds and jungle on the other. Behind Le Corbusier's idea of a city rose the far-off hazy backdrop of the first 7,000-foot ridge of the Himalayas – above that, above the clouds, an ethereal whiteness of snow. Chandigarh is not a slap in the face for the mountains, like the bullying Soviet buildings in the Caucasus, but a tentative half-fearful wave in their direction, respectful, submissive. Fatehpur Sikri, Auroville, Chandigarh: all these are cities in the Indian tradition. A series of beginnings; a series of ruins. The names of so many ideal cities whispered into the sand. The remains of six cities round Delhi. The temples at Mahabalipuram engulfed by the sea. 'It is like reading of a land [wrote Philip Woodruff of India's fatal want of continuity] periodically devastated by hordes of lemmings or locusts, the depressing chronicle of a succession of castles built on the waste land of the sea shore.' Sunset ruins and strident vulgarity: the Brindavan Dam Gardens after Seringapatam; the juke-box in its corner of the hermit's cell. There is room for both, in the space left vacant in the Indian head by the absence of logic.

The last seventy miles or so into the hills took more than three hours of hairpin bends and steep ascent. This was hard work for David. The road, tortuous and rough, showed us steeps and gorges clad with deodar and Himalayan oak, and misty heights and plunging drops. Darkness fell. We reached our goal, 'Honington', above Simla and above Mashobra, at eight o'clock.

We got out of the car. Darkness, whispering trees. The cold was desperate. Lights, salaams – our arrival created in a moment the turmoil of an opened ants' nest as the many servants sent up from Faridkot rushed hither and thither with lanterns wobbling out their shadows into the dark. In we went, looking for warmth. The cold in that gabled wooden cottage was the most intense indoor cold I have ever felt, chilling its way through cashmere and tweed, chilling the marrow of my bones like the pressure of ice closing in on the hull of a doomed vessel. David bustled about giving orders for fires in every room, and we ate our supper in front of a crackling blaze; but the grip of ice was not loosened. Later, in my bedroom, the flames in the grate seemed not to have the power to convey heat through the crystal air, or to warm its icy dampness. I loaded my whole wardrobe on to my bed and crept under the load. Still the cold rasped my throat. A few weeks before, that night in the electric rock garden in Mysore, the heat had been 100 degrees. It was all India, I told myself as I fell asleep, every extreme, every contradiction, every opposite was within India still. Admitting the mixture all together, flame and ice, hermit and juke-box, was the only way to understand it all.

Heavy knocking on my door announced the arrival, next morning, not only of bed-tea but also of a caravan of servants who carried in a hip-bath and hot water in two brass jugs wrapped in towels, which they set before a fire soon rekindled with spitting pine. Shutters were opened. Outside, in the ringing stillness of the mountains, the sunlight of a cold and beautiful morning fell in shafts through the deodars onto a moss lawn pale from its snow cover and sparkling with little blue flowers. The servants withdrew. I looked from under my eiderdown at the hip-bath and hot water. The 1970s had been spirited away in the night and the 1930s brought back in their place.

The substitution suited David. Of the various translations of him that I had known – the David of England and of our European tour as well as the Tikka Sahib of Delhi and Faridkot – it was a new-to-me persona, the laird of 'Honington', which emerged from his quarters that morning. I soon learned that to him this make-believe place, these five family houses 11,000 feet up a mountain – the whole artificial construction of a British hill-station – formed not a curiosity from the past but the preferred option of present-day reality. Nannied by a flutter of servants he swept out through the porte-cochère to a waiting US army jeep, its driver hunkered down beside it in that attitude of tireless patience which outwaits the comings and goings of sahibs white or brown. David drove. Diana and I had seats.

The rest clung on. If the careless grandeur of our progress had a focus, it was in the jeep's number plate, which was scarlet, a Ruler's privilege now disallowed. David's humble Delhi car flaunted no such unwise distinction, but here in the mountains the clock could safely be put back.

David's satisfaction increased with every unlocked door into each deep-frozen house, and with every servant's devoted greeting. With each step backwards into British India he regained his element, like a fish which flips itself back into the pool. In his father's chief residence, 'Kenilworth', a large blue wooden structure bulging out into wings and balconies under an iron roof, we were met by a blanket-swathed old man, terribly thin, with a bunch of keys in his knotted hand. David indicated him without introducing us. 'My father's librarian will show you the library.' I followed this bent and bony elder into ever-colder regions of the house until he stopped in front of a glass-fronted bookcase of considerable size. Within were worn cloth-bound volumes, each spine coarsely stamped with an accession number, which filled the shelves with a precision only to be achieved in a library untroubled by readers. It was the collection of an English soldier, bought (so David told me) by His Highness when he bought the house: books of Asiatic travel, accounts of incidents and actions in the Great Game, memoirs of soldiers and explorers – books in which the British, in short, explained Asia to one another. I asked to have the case opened. The librarian wagged his head, looked across the room at David. 'His Highness is not letting me keep the key of this fellow,' he said, '*very* good books.' 'In a sense', said David quickly, 'over here is the up-to-date section of my father's library.' He sat waiting by a few open shelves. I crossed the floor and looked. Beside Maud Diver's works and some ragged paperbacks was a run of Collins' *Aircraft Annual* ending in 1929 and a number of odd volumes of the *RAC Handbook* for motorists in the British Isles.

From 'Kenilworth' the jeep sped through twisty lanes to 'Sherwood', summer home to David's granny. Here too the interior was still and dark and cold. Here too were the leaded lattices and barley-sugar oak of a Surrey cottage built in the 1920s. Here too, on gate-legged tables like those furnishing the English homes of the retired ICS men who had run India, stood a row of signed and silver-framed photographs of grand people having picnics in the hills, snapshots which established a claim to the friendship of viceroys. The same signed photograph of Himself that satisfied the conquerors' minions – the same condescension – satisfied also the subject race.

We weren't left long to explore 'Sherwood' before the jeep carried us ever higher to reach 'Cosy Nook'. Here we drove into a large concrete yard surrounded by coach-houses, where David parked and his chief attendant, Man Singh, sprang off our vehicle giving orders to the sleepyheads issuing from their retreats. Teams formed to roll back the coach-house doors on castors which shrieked into the silence of the mountains. Then one by one the servants pulled dust-sheets off gleaming motorcars like stablemen pulling the rugs off horses. There was a 1948 Rolls, a '51 Bentley, two Mark VII Jaguars, two '48 Packards, some half-cannibalised US jeeps; then there was a row of motor-bikes. 'My father's collection,' said David, strolling towards them with his hands behind his back. I followed him, and Diana rather pensively followed me. It was not really a 'collection', not choice items deliberately assembled: the contents of the garage were the outcome of buying and never selling – for to sell a car would have hinted at indigence, with consequent lowering of prestige and credit. For the same reason HH 'maintained' a 1955 Austin Cambridge in the Savoy garage in London. So possessions accumulated. It was all wealth. Cars, silver and gold meltable into bullion, Purdey guns and Hardy rods, valuable books in a cabinet no one could open, these Mashobra houses themselves – all were treasure in different forms, all were wealth carried up from his shrinking kingdom in the plains to be heaped together in these mountains at the end of the earth, where a last stand for the past might be made with the family's back to the wall of the Himalayas.

I did not know whether Diana drew the same rather ominous inference as I did from David's complacency in this outpost of fantasy. I have said she was pensive, and so throughout our tour she remained. Was this the moment to board a ship so clearly sinking? We drove down to Clark's for lunch in Simla.

To me Simla was an uncomfortable idea, a drab English town squatting on the frail timber-built native village stacked under it into the hillside, the big yellow English church atop it all like a nabob in a rickshaw, the poky Britishness of the streets at once dull and offensive. Diana exclaimed over it, I could see her brighten. Admiring the gloomy pile of Viceregal Lodge, the ugliest building I had seen in the subcontinent, she claimed gaily that some past relation of hers had been 'offered India'. David cleared his throat irritably, said nothing. Though he wanted his English friends to be grand, he didn't like it when their grandeur impinged upon his territory. He would tell others, he would certainly tell me, that Diana's past relation had been offered India; but he didn't like being told himself. I knew that irritated little cough of his, when his toys tried to get out of their boxes to play on their own.

Through the dusk David drove us back in the open jeep to our mountain retreat. Fires burned and the house was warm. Dinner was served to us at a table set comfortably before the sitting-room hearth. Conversation was easy and expansive. I remember Diana and David talking about clothes for a Delhi party, and her describing the dress she had brought from England.

'Poor old Eve,' I said, 'always stuck with worrying about clothes and appearances ever since she first stitched together the fig leaves.'

Not so, Eve's rep replied, women's superficiality went deeper that that. Women when men thought they were only wondering what to wear were really debating who to be in their own eyes for the particular occasion. Women had a choice of might-be identities which men did not.

[177]

'You mean dependent on their escort?' I asked. 'Greenery-yallery for Bunthorne one day, tweed and headscarf for Sporting Sam the next?'

'No,' she said, 'by the time a woman's twenty-five she will have recognised in herself the potential for more than one identity, and when she stands in front of her wardrobe she's debating not how to dress but which self to be.'

Had she stood in front of her suitcase in London wondering which could-be identity to pack for? I didn't ask. There was a silence, broken by David clearing his throat and asking: 'And how are you finding the waiters in your hotel in Delhi now? Any better?'

'Perfectly sweet. They're only little boys really.' Then she added: 'The breakfast waiter is a bit...a bit of a nuisance.'

There was a pause. David twiddled his beard. 'How do you mean, a nuisance?' he asked.

She stuck her chin out: 'Familiar. Rather familiar.'

We were back among the imperial rules and shibboleths of the 1930s, where both of them felt at home.

In my memory one picture abides of David among the mountains. He has taken a fancy to try one the motor-bikes from the 'Cosy Nook' garages, and a machine is wheeled up to him by the *naffa*, Man Singh. David mounts the bike, bounces once or twice to kick-start it with his little London shoe, wobbles forward trailing his feet. 'Anyone care to join me?' It looks precarious. We stand back, watching. He tucks up his feet and quickens the pace. Behind him runs Man Singh, his hands – as large and safe a pair of hands as Mr Goyle's – held out before him to catch David should he fall. In this order, bike accelerating and *naffa* skimming behind, I see them in memory circle the coachyard of 'Cosy Nook' beneath the glint of Himalayan snows.

Thirteen

A return journey never has quite the buoyancy of the journey out, and so it was with our drive back to Delhi. We came down from the hills into the heat, the fierce hot light of the plains. I was very soon leaving India. The shadow of departure made time spent unprofitably feel like time wasted altogether of what little store remained. When a puncture delayed us at a 'Puncher' shop I walked to and fro through the debris of an Indian roadside between a stone-crushing plant and a pitiable camel, trying as I walked to still the regretful restlessness I felt. Why had I not seen more, followed leads, travelled further? Tea was offered us by the repairers' overseer from the door of his shed, but David would not let us accept. He put himself in charge, and imposed discipline as if we were an expeditionary force in hostile territory. Later, when we had stopped in the outskirts of Ambala to buy a new inner tube and were waiting for a wheel change, Diana said to me 'I'm going for a wander. Come for a wander?' 'No,' called David sharply, 'I don't advise that.'

Why was a wander inadvisable? I thought of that assurance on my rooftop in Pondicherry: 'You just walk out the door. India'll take care of you.' Why should David, who scoffed at others for attributing dangers to India, fear for the safety of the memsahib in Ambala? Or at the hands of her breakfast waiter in Delhi? Diana didn't need protection. But she saw David's need to be her protector, and knuckled under – for the present – to that. She didn't go for her 'wander'; instead she settled placidly into the back seat of the car.

The time to show strength soon came. We were buzzing along in the dark near Kurukshetra, Diana still taking her turn in the back seat, David claiming – as we passed line after line of unlighted bullock-carts – that (because they were forbidden) there were no bullock-carts on the Grand Trunk Road after dark. Suddenly the car lost speed, drifted, and stopped. David smoothed his moustache.

'What's wrong, David?' The sharp question from the back seat.

'Accelerator kaput.' He purred with laughter, partly a nervous defence against interrogation, partly from his delight in the unexpected, that most likeable quirk in his character.

Diana opened her door. 'Bonnet up please.'

David pulled the catch inside the car. By the time we had got out and joined her, she had her head in the engine. Soft-footed oxen and creaking axles passed by in the dark, brushing us with animal scents. She held out a hand. 'Torch.'

'Half a tick.' David trotted back to the driver's door and fished out a torch which he put in her outstretched hand. David carried the equipment which enabled people to do jobs for him, which was the substitute in India for carrying servants. He and I clustered round the raised bonnet under which the torch-beam searched. Walkers and bicyclists turned curious faces on us, and a few feet away, down the road's centre, the public carriers charged behind the lances of their headlights.

Diana's head appeared out of the engine. 'Floss. Find my nightcase. Blue. There's a sponge-bag. Floss. Bring it will you.'

David looked at me uncertainly, caught out. 'Floss?'

'Dental floss,' I whispered, trying to pull him out of the target area before another bullet hit him.

He stumbled back in. 'Is it toothpaste?'

Rapid fire on both of us. 'Oh, one of you, just bring me my sponge-bag will you.'

We hastened to take luggage from the boot, found her neat 'boxes', located the sponge-bag, took it to our leader. Telling David to hold the torch steady she looked out her dental floss, cut off a length with convenient scissors and disappeared under the bonnet, the beam of light on her busy hands. In a minute or so she straightened. 'Accelerator cable. Parted, but I've fixed it up. Should last to Delhi. Got a rag, David?'

David found a rag to clean her hands. I dropped the bonnet with a feeling that I was letting fall the curtain on an allegorical drama. We reloaded the luggage, climbed aboard and continued towards Delhi. I remember a thoughtful silence. She could not altogether suppress her capabilities. She had revealed her hand, and it was a strong one, practical, workmanlike – but masculine. Too strong. In an emergency, under the red riding-hood of meek obedience, she was found to be wearing the SAS rescue outfit. The Incident at Kurukshetra made her formidable. David could dodge playing chess against her, but sooner or later he faced a contest he could not avoid and would not win. I foresaw that in that *mauvais quart d'heure* beside the Grand Trunk Road she had as good as hanged herself with her own dental floss.

My time too was up. A few more evenings of parties and farewells full of Indian confidence that India had hooked me – 'I'll wager you'll be back to join up with us next cold-weather' – which I knew it had, and believed that I would. I meant to go back. Then early one morning my plane lifted off from Palam, leaving David to settle back gratefully into Jorbagh routine while I flew west into a Europe parched by winter. Ahead lay a house we were to take possession of in a few days' time, and a first-born child due in a month. A new life. I watched the dawn unwrap desert kingdoms below the plane, and 'wondered if India ever were real'.

David did not belong in the future. He came in September of that year to stay with us, and he and I amused ourselves as we had always done. The future had hardly begun. We were in our new home, and our new baby slept in his nursery upstairs, but neither the house nor the child had yet put forth their strength. Downstairs in the front rooms, or on our trip for a few days to a Bath hotel, it was still possible for me to masquerade as the friend David had always known.

[181]

By the date of his next visit to England, three years later, there was no use pretending the future hadn't arrived and settled down for good. Our son was three, and a new baby had been born that year. What had been tentative at the time of David's first visit had in three years become custom and habit. I had evolved out of the person he knew into rural middle age. When he wrote in advance of his coming I did not reply. When he rang from London I arranged to meet him for lunch the following week. The day came, a fine September morning, a settled landscape outside my dressing-room window, a settled programme before me of writing and gardening and playing with children, which I did not want to disturb. I did not want to put on London clothes. I rang the house where David was staying, knowing it was too early to find him awake, and left a message to say I had missed the train.

David's mistrustful vigilance, which sought to draw the sting of betrayal by expecting it, had caused him to set up a fall-back plan, or at any rate a cover story, for the lunch we had been supposed to share. More than a year later a letter came on Faridkot's crested writing paper, the glueless Indian stamps as usual stuck on with scraps of tape:

My dear Philip,

Delighted to have had your letter. I have taken so long in replying for as per your instructions I had to obtain a copy of *Heat and Dust* first. Apparently our censors did not think too highly of the references to the Mother Country and it was only after much head-scratching that they finally allowed the locals to read it. I enjoyed it immensely and thought Mrs J had sized up beautifully the role of the ICS and the importance of Simla but did not ring true on the Kitty/Kavin bit. As far as I know, of the 276 'rulers' of which all but about 20 of the original signatories of the 'Instrument of Accession' are dead, not one of them or their direct heirs lives permanently in a flat in South Ken or for that matter anywhere outside India. 'Visits' yes – as often as poss! – but we still seem to think there is so much going on for us here that prevents 'foreign residence' – ostrich-like maybe, but that's the way it is.

Sorry to have missed you in London in September. Peters brought up the sad news along with the breakfast tray...however, as it was then only about 10 am I hastened to the telephone and accepted [a friend's] invitation to lunch at White's. I came away with the impression that it was very much a sort of adult version of the Pitt Club. Stomachs were more distended, hairs greyer, but still the same stubborn tendency to be one of the boys. While in London – largely because Santosh, an old school and Cantab chum was there – I played a lot of *le ping-pong électronique* and was reminded of our games together. Have you played much since? The new machines (and I refer to circa Aug/Sept 1976) are vastly more complicated.

This summer I did a month's trip to the sultry South. We had a house in the Nilgiris which formed the base and it was all rather different from North India. For instance the servants still call you 'Master' and serve you steak and kidney pud with as little difficulty as they would have over a 'Rogan-Josh' up North.

The Heinz sisters who were lunching yesterday squeaked with delight when your name was mentioned...'Is he coming over this cold-weather?' they asked. I do wish you would.

Love

DAVID

I never saw him again; it was not only in my future that David didn't belong, he had no future of his own either. There was no Fair Haven at the end of the lane. In a very few years he was dead, of cirrhosis of the liver. Last reports of him in Delhi describe a decline that was steep and dreadful.